The World
Of Art-
The World
Of Youth

Paul A. Schreivogel

The World Of Art- The World Of Youth

**A PRIMER ON THE USE OF ARTS
IN YOUTH MINISTRY**

**DESIGN AND ILLUSTRATION
ROBERT FRIEDERICHSEN**

Augsburg Publishing House
Minneapolis, Minnesota

THE WORLD OF ART—THE WORLD OF YOUTH
Copyright © 1968 Joint Youth Publications Council
All rights reserved
Library of Congress Catalog Card No. 68-13430

Manufactured in the United States of America

The World Of Art The World Of Youth

Contents

FOR . . .

E. A. Zeile
Ron Redder
    . . . two servanthood pastors
Dave Wurm
    . . . a sensitive youth minister
St. Paul Lutheran Church
    . . . its youth ministry
The basement room of St. Paul's
    . . . where this manuscript was written

TE DEUM . . .

The World Of Art— The World Of Youth

THE IDEA OF THIS BOOK

This book is intended for the congregation's ministry. Although it is partially oriented toward those who work with young people, it may be used as a resource for the entire ministry of the congregation. (The ideas and concepts presented here can create settings in which members of the congregation may respond freely to one another in the joy and challenge of being Christian in God's creation.) Youth advisors working with this material will gain a deeper appreciation of the worlds of youth as the youth and the adults share a ministry to one another.

Of equal value is the establishment of lines of communication between adults, as well as youth and adults. Using art as the central form, a common language can be shaped in which theological issues and concerns of life are shared among Christian people.

We are not concerned here with what is usually labeled "Christian Education." Rather, we are dealing with a process of growth in which members of the community of believers share their life, thoughts, goals, and faith with one another in order to prepare and sustain themselves for their life in the world where God wants his people to live and to serve.

The arts and the church have been hand-in-glove partners since creation— sometimes more readily accepted by one another than at others. The recent surge of sensitivity to the arts in our country is calling the church to renew its ties with the arts. Young people, particularly, are living in the world of the arts, as a survey of any average high school will readily confirm. And this book is designed to aid the adults of a congregation in understanding the perception and involvement of young people in the arts, and help in training young people to be perceptive as their lives intersect with books, films, television, comics, and music.

THE ART FORM

It is difficult to offer a precise definition for an art form or its use. Much depends upon one's perspective. A "purist" may have a very sensitive and precise definition of what art is and how it is to be used; but questions related to art and its forms call neat definitions into question. For instance: Is a symphony orchestra performing a Bach selection an art form in itself? Is the performance a work of art as well as the composition? Is a young person who spends months perfecting the engine and the body styling of a hot-rod participating in an art? If he calls this hot-rod "The Kandy-Kolored, Tangerine-Flaked, Streamlined Baby," is it the name of an art form?

For the purpose of this book we shall define an art form as "an artistic approach to life in which the creator of the form desires to address humanity." The art form may take shape as writing, painting, carving, welding, acting, constructing, etc. Essentially the art form, no matter which is used, is telling us something about ourselves as it depicts or celebrates a facet of life.

The art form assists people to see life in their times. Some art forms evoke evil and have the demonic within them. Other forms share the acts of God as they celebrate God's movement in history. As the artist takes a serious look at the world and society he forces Christian people into reflection and discussion concerning their role as the people of God in the world. As the Christian participates in both styles of art—demonic and celebration—he is to reflect upon his role as the perceptive servant of God in a world in need of God's message and action in Christ.

Christ's prayer for his disciples in John 17 offers a clue for our mission, "I am not praying that you will take them out of the world but that you will keep them from the evil one." In order that members of the congregation, particularly youth, may be lights in the world they must perceive God at work in the world as well as "the evil one." The art form can assist in this perception process.

ART AS COMMUNICATION MEDIA

Though intended for young people, this book is aimed at placing members of the congregation in settings which enable them, under the power of the Gospel, to distinguish what is truth in what they see and hear every day. The art forms in this book are for the purpose of establishing lines of communication, that is, freeing people in relationship to talk about and share their life and their God in forms a group can understand. In this manner the art form is neither a "gimmick" nor a "visual aid," but an occasion which may precipitate a relationship in which communication, understanding, and love take place.

Our society is undergoing a transformation in symbols and language. These

Introduction

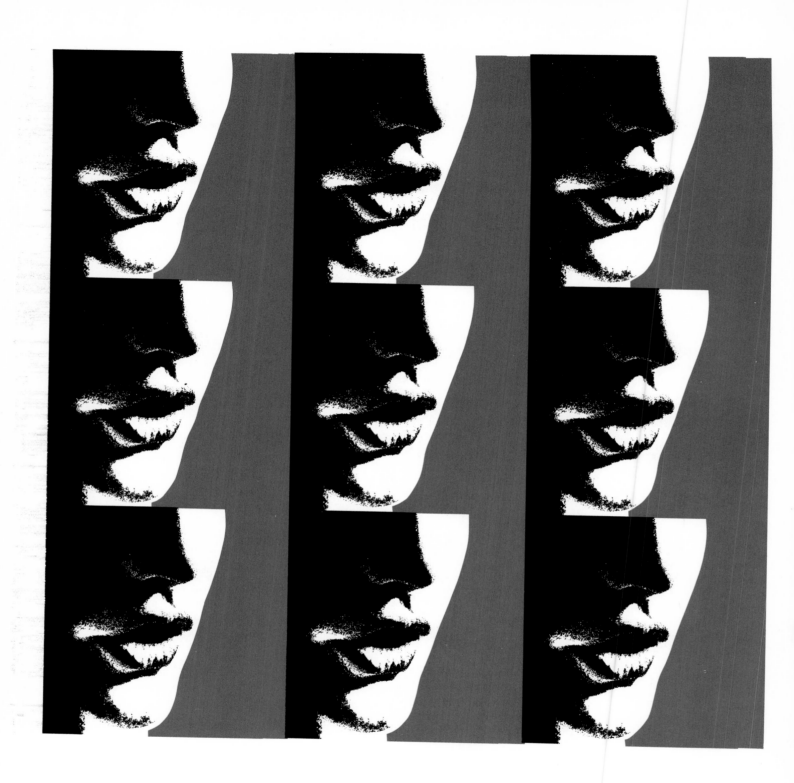

8

are changing with each generation. Communication in the life-style of a group of people implies a mutual knowledge and understanding of their mode of communication as well as the hidden meanings behind their communication forms. When an art form is shared together it serves, indirectly, to open a group for relationship in which a common language can be achieved. Words which people know and understand can be wedded to the shared experience of these people.

Perhaps a simple example of the difficulty of attempted communication can be demonstrated by use of the word "peace" (pax). There is a vast difference in meaning communicated by this word in the following four situations: (a) in its original theological context, (b) as it is normally used by a church body or a congregation, (c) as nations use the word, and (d) as it is used by political parties and backyard neighbors. When the word "peace" is used in a group it is necessary to discover what the user means by the word. An assumption that people are receiving the meaning which the user desires to communicate simply because he speaks the word "peace" is obviously incorrect, yet this kind of misunderstanding occurs regularly in the churches' pulpits and pews. It simply demonstrates the communication problem of our age. Visual arts can assist in breaking down the communication barriers.

ART FORMS IN THIS BOOK
The art forms which are introduced on the following pages, though not all-inclusive, are taken from the worlds of youth. The use of these forms in the church will help equip young people for their ministry by enabling them to talk and apply their stance under the Gospel in the world.

Groups in varying geographical and social areas will have their own particular emphasis or concern relating to the art form. For that reason it is necessary that each group seek how its own youth are so exposed. A key source for seeking out the involvement of young people in the arts is the local high school. Other avenues include observation of such sources as *Time, Life, Newsweek, Saturday Review, Seventeen, Mad,* American Library Association, community library, etc. It should not be assumed that the adults know what young people are seeing, hearing, and talking. They may need to be alerted to their youth through these resources in order to understand the world of youth.

CREATION AND YOUTH
The world is undergoing radical changes which the arts readily reflect. It is important that both adults and youth recognize that these changes are not all evil. In fact, it is of the very excitement of faith to see and recognize the avenues of God's grace loose in the world as we move to new discoveries. At the same time that Christians see God's grace in the dynamic changes and discoveries in the world, they should also see it in the common, at the supermarket and the drug store. Although evil is present, at the same time God is in the world and continues his acts of creation. Christians must be perceptive to evil, but they must also have eyes open when God "moves in."

As the Christian lives out his life of joy and hope it is his task to bring the Gospel to every situation, be it coming alive to his role through the media of art and the Word, or serving others as he lives out life in the marketplace. The Christian is called to celebrate—to dance—in the midst of good and evil. Why?—because Christ *has* overcome all —HURRAH!

"Good Grief"

"The true humorist does not hide. He searches for the hidden absurdities, the implicit pomposities, and he puts the bright light of daytime on them. Chaplain has said: 'What is humor? It is a kind of gentle and benevolent custodian of the mind that prevents us from being overwhelmed by the apparent seriousness of life.'"

(*Walt Kelly*, The New York Times).

The cartoon and the comic strip have been a part of our national scene for many years. They have been taken for granted and are so common to our daily life that we have generally neglected them. Rarely have people considered comics as significant art forms, yet for years the comics through their unique style have expounded many causes and have been crammed with social commentary. Often we have rebelled against the "trash" in comics and missed the potent opportunities they offer for insights, both theological and social.

Young people are avid fans of the comics for good reason, for comics often incorporate the best qualities of the adolescent style of life (idealism, irritation with the status quo, etc.) and thereby reflect a quality richly needed in a society possessed by the importance of impersonal computers and efficiency experts.

VISUAL FOLK ART

Comics have been called the "visual folk art." They are the oldest and most enduring popular art form in America. Their popularity stems from many causes. No doubt they serve as an escape from daily routine, offer easy identification with particular individuals and political causes, and appeal to our basic emotions. But whatever the reason, the comics remain important to our daily routine. No popular daily newspaper is without its comic page, and one need only observe the reading habits of the commuters on train, subway, or bus to recognize that comics are read as intently as the front page. The function and potential influence in our society of the comic strip, as well as its effect on the lives of Christian people, demand that it be taken seriously.

The comics generally reflect society; they mirror the life around them. Some have called the comics the "proletarian novels of America" because so many of the comics deal with ordinary people in ordinary life situations. What many of us may not realize, however, is that comics and cartoonists dig beneath the ordinary actions of life and find deeper meaning to our style of living. Many cartoonists are serious students of theology, psychology, medicine, and other fields of social dynamics. Perhaps it is because they take people so seriously that the comics have an uncanny ability to relate in a human way to young people and are so popular with them.

This visual folk art struggles to become recognized as an art form in this country. At the International Convention of Comics in Italy, 1965, a critic made the following remark to the noted American cartoonist, Al Capp: "Classifying comics as a subculture is a form of prejudice you Americans will never overcome." Capp's terse reply was, "We shall overcome."

For many years Europe has had groups and organizations which meet regularly to discuss the meaning and message of the cartoon.

CRITICISM AND LAUGHTER

A cartoonist simply draws things on paper and lets us look at them. The pictures he draws will mean different things to different people. Fortunately the innate ability of the comics to make us laugh, often at ourselves, makes the comics less menacing and more amusing. We are more ready to accept criticism when that criticism is couched in humor, evoking a healthy attitude in the ability to laugh at the serious. Faith, confidence, and trust seem to mark the individual who can laugh at humor expressed about serious values "in spite of . . . ." For that very reason the Christian who is urged to "open eyes and see" must not overlook the thrust and seriousness of the comics. They enable us to view the world and ourselves from a different perspective. They offer a verbal-visual humor which carries a punch, though it sometimes hurts. Many of the serious ones (*Peanuts, Pogo, Li'l Abner,* Feiffer) are serious enough to study as well as laugh at.

A LOOK AT SOME COMICS
Li'l Abner (Al Capp)

Li'l Abner delves into political satire, besides adding Lower Slobbovia to our geographical language. Li'l Abner drew its strength and popularity out of the New Deal days of the 30's. Capp's characters are the aristocrats of a backwoods society where the people and their lives are rigidly defined. The Dogpatch life-style is wild with everyone going all-out all the time. The Yokum family is a powerful group, but their power is held in check by their common decency. With them cartoonist Capp has attacked what he defines as socialism (the schmoos), attempted to solve the evil people commit against one another (the kigmies—"what our country needs is a good five-cent masochist"), and has spot-lighted government spending and power as well as the evils of big business.

The hero of the strip is Li'l Abner, a simple, illiterate hillbilly, yet the pronounced enemy of all that is evil in the

Comics

world. Li'l Abner is a David facing the world's Goliaths. Al Capp has been one of the oldest and best political satirists in the country.

Pogo (Walt Kelly)

Walt Kelly accomplishes the same task as Al Capp but he does it by using back-woods swamp animals and a style that is not as blatant as Li'l Abner. Interestingly, the characters of *Pogo* run counter to the traditional natural role of the swamp animal. The least noble is a cigar-smoking alligator (does he smoke to break his meat-eating habit?); the least sensible is the opossum; the least arrogant is a worm. The wrongness of the characters seems to liberate them from their traditional image and make them funnier. Walt Kelly is a master satirist, and no one is spared his pen. The minute someone is taken seriously in society, and in a sense becomes godlike, Kelly reaches for his pen. He is not afraid to speak about serious matters or to engage these matters through humor and satire. His topics have covered such items as presidential elections, demonstrations, McCarthyism, Communism, the world series, the John Birch Society (Jack Acid Society), and a host of other political and social concerns. Perhaps, someday, Kelly and Capp will comment on the organized church!

Miss Peach (Mell Lazarus)

This strip takes place with small sophisticated children in a school community. The advent of progressive education gave us *Miss Peach*. It deals with smug little children who show up their elders, brainwash one another, and constantly practice one-up-manship.

B.C. (Johnny Hart)

Johnny Hart reflects upon modern life through the eyes of cro-magnon cave-men, sharp-shooting anteaters, and terrified ants.

Rex Morgan, Apartment 3-G, Judge Parker (Dr. Nick Dallis)

These three comic strips are learning situation stories offering insight into medicine, psychiatry, and law. They are written by the same author (using a pseudonym). Strangely enough, different artists draw the strips, one drawing the characters, the other filling in the background. A survey conducted in 1965 found these three comic strips very popular with young people. They have been called the comic strip "soap operas."

Judge Parker is a slow moving drama offering studies in sociology and law.

Rex Morgan, M.D. avoids issues of controversy such as Medicare and birth control, but does provide drama with a good deal of medical insight and accuracy.

Apartment 3-G relates the stories of women who are husband-hunting. The girls do very little in terms of contributions to society.

Dick Tracy, Little Orphan Annie

These are comic strips which may be called the advance guard of the Pop Art movement.

In *Dick Tracy* we always find good triumphing over evil, and any means are justifiable to that end. Chester Gould, the creator of this comic strip, occasionally takes sideswipes at current social happenings. A 1967 story featured this comment by a captured criminal in the strip, "You can't get me, copper! You can't violate my constitutional rights!"

Little Orphan Annie is the story of the ageless little girl seeking good in an evil world. This comic strip is a nightmare of clichés. Annie reminds us of the Perils of Pauline. She can always be found in the safe hands of big industrialists, and the strip seems to convey an ultraconservative tone.

War Comic Strips

These comics are most popular in time of military conflict. The recent Viet Nam happenings have again boosted the traditional strips of *Terry and the Pirates, Steve Canyon,* and *Buz Sawyer. Tales of the Green Berets* fills the public's interest in battlefield strategy (plus a good dose of propaganda).

Peanuts (Charles Schulz)

The present interest of the church in the comics received impetus from the publication of the book *The Gospel According to Peanuts,* by Robert Short (John Knox Press). Since the book appeared churches throughout the country have been taking a look at the world of *Peanuts.*

Peanuts came upon the American scene in 1950 as a space filler in nine newspapers. Since that time it has been pinned or pasted on more office bulletin boards, locker rooms, and pastors' studies than any of its predecessors. Some people have indicated it should also be pinned to the church pew. It is now the most universally popular comic strip in existence, appearing in more than 700 newspapers in 1967.

In this comic strip we are introduced to children who are caricatures of adults. The children are not mischief-makers nor are they in conflict with adults (as in *Dennis the Menace, Captain and the Kids,* etc.). The community of *Peanuts* is one which sharply reflects our life and world as well as the adult style of living. In fact, *Peanuts* is unique in that it utilizes an adult frame of reference in a situation totally populated by children.

Peanuts does not rely on humor as much as on the personal interpretation an individual gives to the subject which is treated. Charles Schulz, creator of *Peanuts,* stated in a television interview: "I draw *Peanuts* from ideas in my head and my life, and I let the people interpret." Here we see the psychological

reflection of contemporary life, one that ultimately seems to say: "Happiness is the agony of self doubt" ("Lord, I believe, help thou my unbelief").

A word about some of the characters of *Peanuts:*

Charlie Brown—Charlie Brown is the born loser of the *Peanuts* community; he is a "nowhere man." He never does anything mean, but he is weak and vulnerable. He is the "New York Mets" of the comics, the "Buster Keaton" of the cartoon world, a born loser. Charlie struggles to gain acceptance by the community of *Peanuts;* he seeks identity of self as a human person; he desires the feeling of success, of worthiness (someday he'll get the kite to fly, beat Lucy at checkers, and throw the ball into the basket as does Linus). Theologians have read out of Charlie Brown the struggle of man with "original sin" and alienation. Others see him as a signal for the "decline of the American male." People laugh at Charlie Brown because in Charlie they see a bit of themselves.

Lucy—Lucy is the intellectual of the group. She represents the educated and domineering American female who frequently calls upon the female attributes of the slow sulk, temper tantrum, and loud voice in order to get her way. She is the Ayn Rand of the community, the original "rugged individualist" who has no doubts about where she is going and how she is going to get there. With her background of education (nursery school, picnic school, and hopefully, military school) she constantly humiliates Charlie Brown. Lucy is a product of "the establishment" and constantly confuses her community with her twisted logic.

Schroeder—Schroeder is the thorn in the flesh for Lucy. He is the only male able to outdo her, and thereby he is the hope of the American male. Schroeder also typifies the role of the artist in society. When Lucy calls him to play

"Three Blind Mice" for a birthday party, Schroeder replies, "Only three years old and already I'm forced to go commercial."

Linus—All the characters of *Peanuts* have security fetishes, but the blatant example of reliance on a false god is Linus. His blanket symbolizes the false idols and hopes found in each of us. Linus is so tied to his idol that he says, "When I grow up I'm going to turn my blanket into a coat." His blanket reminds us of the things we hope will make us happy, but don't. The members of the *Peanuts* community are always urging Linus to go through the process of "withdrawal" from his blanket and to stand on his own two feet.

Snoopy—The "non-human" in the *Peanuts* group is a dog. Robert Short refers to Snoopy as "the hound of heaven." It is easy to read into the character of Snoopy the way of the typical Christian, or at least what a Christian should be. Snoopy struggles with the problems of indecision and pain in his life; he is subject to frequent humiliation by the community (suffering servant?); he wonders why he is different— a dog (a "chosen" dog, a "royal" dog, a "called out" dog—First Peter); he attacks the false security of Linus. Above all, Snoopy seems to have a concept of joy and celebration. The gang of *Peanuts* cannot quite understand Snoopy's brazen act of dancing. They chide him for dancing; they raise questions about dancing in the midst of famine and flood; they call him stupid; *but* he still dances. He seems to say to us that the Christian life is one of celebration of the acts of God in our lives; and ultimately, in the midst of chaos and death, all the Christian can do is celebrate what Christ has done and is doing in the midst of his life; claiming the victory over death and the demonic. Snoopy is "Zorba the Greek" of the *Peanuts* world.

The comic *Peanuts* is open to various types of interpretations. A reading of *The Gospel According to Peanuts* and a collection of *Peanuts* comic strips may lead a group to a healthy and interesting discussion of the role of the Christian as a person and as a member of the community. Interesting discussions could revolve around the meaning of the continual appearance of the "tree" in the strip, or the "Great Pumpkin."

THE CARTOONISTS

Many authors and artists offer their material and comment through single cartoons or panels. Among these are:

Jules Feiffer—Feiffer is a humorist of the first order. Through the use of a minimum of pictures and large captions he presents a tragi-comedy of life. Feiffer writes and draws to suit himself; he does not write to please the trinity of the newspaper syndicate, editors, or readership. His classic monologues and dialogues are found in books of his own cartoons or in Sunday supplements and a few daily newspapers. It takes courage to enjoy Feiffer, for he deals in areas of extreme sensitivity, often flaying each of us with his twitchy lines, very long dialogues, and multiple drawings. Feiffer is truly "sick, sick, sick" (title of one of his cartoon books) if this means having sensitivity for and sharp insight into an age of the "power of positive thinking." One may disagree with Feiffer in his interpretations of our world, but he offers a breath of fresh air in his messages to each person. He speaks in a psychological, sociological, and theological framework.

William Steig—Steig offers a sensitive approach to life through visuals and text which often display sorrow and ridiculous situations.

Robert Osborn—Many people are not acquainted with Osborn. His books, with wild and strange figures which seem to

such a service to congregations. The second is by using television as an art form. Careful selection of movies, dramatic programs, and documentaries will enable a group to meet and discuss the program viewed.

Hopefully the future will see the church influencing television with creative programming as well as members of the church being perceptive to the influence for good or evil found in television viewing.

TELEVISION AND YOUNG PEOPLE

Young people are viewing television (15,000 hours from birth to high school graduation). It is as much a part of their life as radio was for an earlier generation. Educators believe television is no detriment to young people. Many of them insist that television does not detract from wholesome recreation but, rather, keeps young people away from unwholesome activities. Others indicate that better students generally view more television than do mediocre students, and that television viewing has increased the reading habits of young people, particularly in the non-fiction field.

There are, of course, some risks to be run. Not the least of these for youth is exposure to the premium placed on glibness and "personality." The use of TV viewing as a part of the church's structured program for young people can counter such influences with sharpened perspective and offer occasions for understanding.

USING TELEVISION

1. Announce significant television programs through church communication media such as Sunday bulletins and church papers. (*Mass Media Ministries* is an excellent guide—see *Resources.*)

2. Form a study group to view and study television programs. Consider the meaning of the material in terms of the Christian life. The discussion guides from the Film section of this book may be used as a basis for group conversation. Note particularly what types of value and moral decisions are depicted in the program. Study the commercials. To what do the commercials appeal? What do commercials imply if one does not use a particular product? Do the commercials speak of the "meaning of man" in a subliminal manner?

3. Some youth groups have written television dramas and submitted them to local television stations or church television departments. Some churches have purchased video taping equipment for the purpose of taping television programs for later showing with various congregational groups. Others have used the video taping units for producing their own television dramas. A good video taping outfit will cost approximately $1,500.

4. Many television networks offer their successful programs to the public on 16mm film. These films can be received for a small rental fee or simply the mailing cost.

5. The national networks are concerned about viewers' reaction to programming, both positive and negative comments. If one desires to comment on programming, or wishes to receive a program on film for viewing, he may write to the following networks:

NBC, 30 Rockefeller Plaza, New York 10020
ABC, 1330 Avenue of the Americas, New York 10019
CBS, 51 West 52nd Street, New York 10019

Television is a gift to be used wisely and with purpose. Be willing to discuss the merits and demerits of shows you have viewed with other people. Be ready to defend the quality and the wisdom of your selectivity.

20

RESOURCES

Television and Radio, Tyler Poyntz, editor. H. W. Wilson Co., 1961. (Collection of magazine articles related to radio and television.)

The People Look at Television, Gary A. Steiner, Alfred A. Knopf. 1963. (A report of a study at the Bureau of Applied Social Research, Columbia University.)

The Television Dilemma, Yale Roe. Hastings House, 1962.

Understanding Media: The Extensions of Man, Marshall McLuhan. McGraw-Hill Paperbacks, 1965.

Mass Media Ministries (see *Film* resource list).

U.S. Office of Education (HEW), Washington, D.C., Educational Media Branch.

Television Information Office (TIO)
The Television Information Office was established in 1959 to provide a bridge between the television industry and the public. TIO is supported by ABC, NBC, CBS, individual commercial and educational stations, and the National Association of Broadcasters. Its aim is to assist the general public as well as professional people (librarians, educators, clergy, etc.) with research and information related to television. TIO maintains an extensive library related to the cultural and sociological aspects of television. TIO offers material to the public free of charge. For a brochure listing materials available write to:

Television Information Office
745 Fifth Avenue
New York, New York 10022

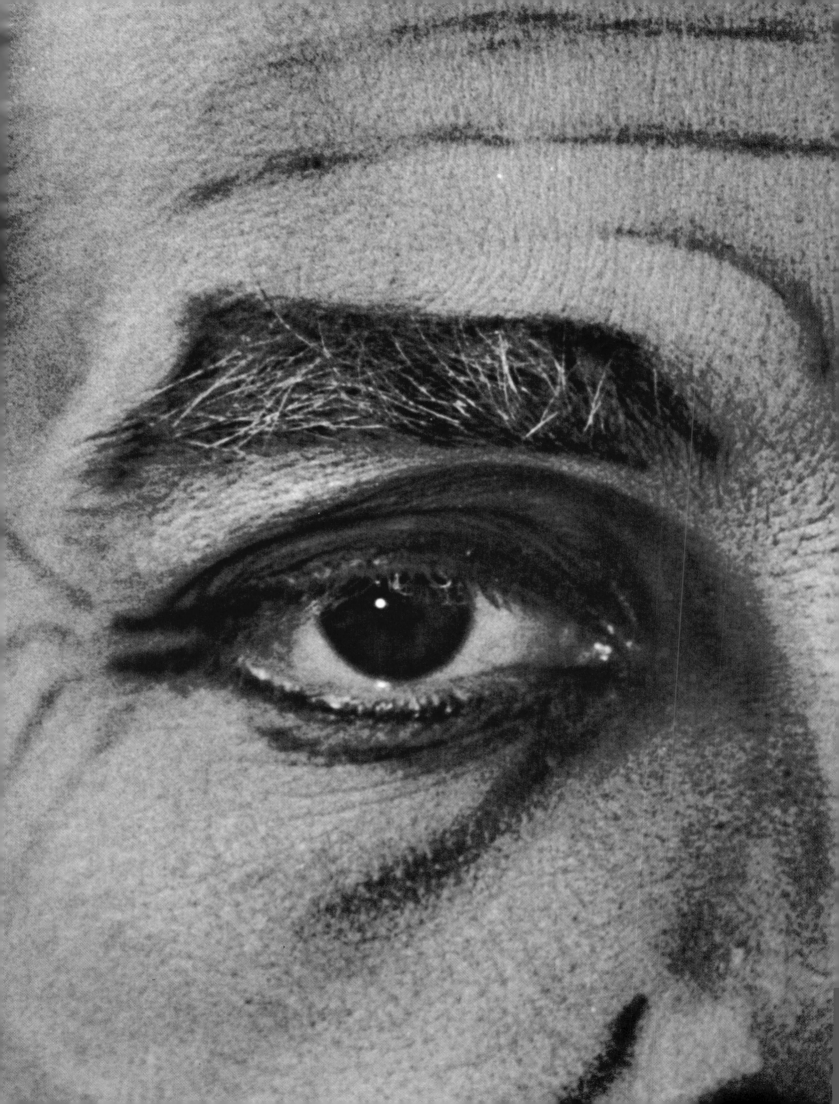

Focus On The Film

"I just sort of get aggravated when I talk to people who don't consider film as an art form. Films have more going on than other mediums and this is the art that I think is going to dominate."
                                    (18-year-old student)

"Films have opened up and enlightened me to others." This comment by a high school person reflects a new phenomenon of our age, the visually oriented person. In the past, instruction and growth came chiefly by the printed page, by books, pamphlets, newspapers, and magazines. From the time of Gutenberg the world has been developing in a literate age. Now, in the 20th century, something new has been added, the communication forms of the visual. The birth of television and the maturing of the film have moved the world into a new cycle of history. No longer does a young person develop only as a literate being, but also as a *cinematic* person because the visual has created a new language form composed of speech, sound effects, angle shots, editing, lighting, and other motifs.

A recent study has shown that from birth to high school graduation the average young person in our society will have viewed approximately 15,000 hours of television and more than 500 films. The time which he will have spent in academic settings in school and church education programs will amount to about 13,000 hours. The sheer weight of these figures demonstrates the potential power of the visual today in the life of the young.

In a sense the world has now become youth's classroom rather than the classroom being his world. Film and television have given him an open window to the world so that he no longer lives in pro-

tected confines. In the inner-city, rural areas, and suburban communities youth are responding to the visual presentations of twentieth century life. By way of the screen youth can taste war, pain, death, life, joy, sorrow, poverty, ignorance, and hate. They experience the needs of people in a variety of human situations.

No church involved in the nurture and growth of young persons can afford to avoid the film because it is *the* media of young people and because it can, at times, communicate truth better than words or books. Use of the film engenders a spirit of thought and community relationships as discussions develop around the probing images of this art form.

A LOOK AT THE WORLD OF FILMS

The film is an art form unique to the twentieth century. Even though film is still in its infancy, its power to communicate is just being discovered.

From the beginnings of the crude pioneer efforts of Edison's makeshift studios in New Jersey came an art form designed to entertain, excite, irritate, and educate. Charlie Chaplain, Buster Keaton, Mickey Mouse, and Theda Bara gave the film its impetus and acceptance. Its popularity has grown so rapidly that today not only the stars of the film but also great directors like Bergman, Fellini, Nichols, and Antonioni are familiar to youth.

The rise of the film has not gone unnoticed by the church. It is difficult to find a congregation without a 16mm film projector and a screen suspended from some superstructure in the church building. Most church bodies have film departments and commissions, and some have gone into the business of producing films.

Formerly "religious films" were a series of contrived, prosaic efforts, similar to the old time western. The "good guys" and the "bad guys" were easy to identify. Now, however, cliché-ridden plots of the past are giving way to creative new efforts of communicating theological truth about the aliveness of God in our world. The film *Parable*, originally produced for the Protestant Pavilion at the New York World's Fair, 1964-65, is an example of creative work by the church. This film offers an excellent opportunity to discover truths of the Christian life through the symbols and actions of the film.

The commercial films being produced for the theater are beginning to improve in style and content. Many commercial films deal with deeply significant theological issues when they honestly reflect the human situation. The Christian, by nature of his baptism, is forced to view the film through the message of the Gospel and bring a Christian view and interpretation to the film. Regardless of the original intent of the film, the Christian still brings the power and beauty of God to it. For this reason such films as *Zorba the Greek* and *A Thousand Clowns* (celebration and freedom themes); *Lord of the Flies* and *Pawnbroker* (alienation and sin); *Billy Budd* and *The Virgin Spring* (struggle between good and evil); *David and Lisa* and *Lilies of the Field* (human relationships) take on significant Christian concerns and concepts.

It is unfortunate that such creations as *The Greatest Story Ever Told* and other so-called religious films have failed in their attempts to communicate. They are generally films designed to "cash in" on the religious sentiment of people rather than to make a significant contribution or communication. One of the best exceptions to this in recent years was *The Gospel According to St. Mat-*

24

Anthony Quinn and Alan Bates
in a scene from "Zorba the Greek"
printed by permission of International Classics

thew, a film produced, ironically, by a Communist.

Films have been called a new form of modern novel, perhaps more intense than any written form because of their ability to use all forms of art as well as to involve many of the senses of man. If this be true then it becomes increasingly important to develop perception and good taste in films. As tastes improve in the young so will the potentialities be present for improvement of taste in other art forms, including sermons and church services.

Finally, the film offers an opportunity to speak parables and truths in images and language recognized as the communication forms of the twentieth century. The secular experience found in the film helps us to understand that what is true in the Christian's life is true for the life of every man, and that God has spoken to us in our modern human situation through Jesus Christ.

MAKING A FILM — THE UNDERGROUND REVOLUTION

In recent years individuals and groups have discovered the pleasure and excitement of making their own films. In numerous high schools throughout the country film courses have been instituted as part of the English curriculum, resulting in hundreds of young people expressing themselves through the film.

The name given to many of these new experimental creations was "the underground film." They were called "underground" because it was virtually impossible for the general public to see them since they were shown only to close friends or at small film festivals. Most of these films were produced with no scripts or plots and were acted out by friends of the film maker. They would vary in length from three minutes to several hours.

The "underground film" is finally coming to the surface. Many cities have theaters which feature only these films, and many local communities are sponsoring these films at church events. The revolution in the underground film has revealed the potential of this new art form to many people. As a result film production is soaring as an avocation of many ordinary people. Film-making is beginning to rank with painting, writing, woodworking, etc., as an expressive art form and hobby.

Any youth group or individual may discover the excitement of producing a film. It is not as "far out" as it may sound. A group only needs some creativity and a desire for hard work. Often a retreat for the purpose of planning the film is the best way to initiate the project. The following steps should be followed for a successful venture:

1. Equipment needed. The basic equipment is an 8mm camera and a tape recorder if sound is desired. Some camera companies produce special tape recorders with tape which may be added to the 8mm film for sound. The "Super 8" film is in common use and may be the international standard for small films. (A search of the local community may turn up an individual with a 16mm camera. The film and processing costs for 16mm film is much more expensive and should not be attempted until one is acquainted with the techniques of film-making.) A splicer will be needed to eliminate bad shots and shape the film into a format.

2. Study the language of the film. Perhaps a local photographer will instruct the group in such expressive film-making techniques as "panning," "zoom," etc. The group will need to view films as well as television to observe techniques and forms available in shooting their film. The Eastman Kodak Company offers a number of inexpensive books for the film-maker. Most local photography stores sell these materials.

3. Select a director of the film. It will be his task to oversee the entire operation and production of the film. He will work with the committees: props, make-up, cameraman, etc.

4. Develop a budget for the film. Include in the budget the cost of planning sessions, rental of equipment, processing of film, costumes (if any), props, travel expenses and, of course, a corsage for the star of the film at its premiere.

5. Outline the script or plans for the film. Begin by listing the ideas and the possible sequences which could be involved in making the film. Select the final outline, leaving options for change in scenes.

6. Select location for filming as well as characters. If community help is required or filming involves use of public or private property seek the assistance of local authorities.

7. Begin the filming. This will be the most interesting portion of the entire production.

8. Have the film processed. Then begin the editing which is the key work of the film. Tying the segments of the film together and eliminating inferior segments requires time, skill, and patience. One young person took two days to shoot a film and twenty-five hours to edit it.

9. If there is no sound, appropriate pop music may be selected to be played as a background to the film. When the film is completed a "world premiere" may be held at the church or in a home.

The processes listed for making a film are basic. It is advisable to get some professional "clues" from a local photographer or a member of the church who understands the film language. There are many books in the local library and photography stores which are related to film production.

Each year the Eastman Kodak Company sponsors the *Kodak Teen-Age Movie Contest.* This contest is open to young film-makers ages twelve to nineteen. The films may be produced by a single person or a team of young people. For further information contact the high school English or Art department (Kodak sends them information each year) or write to: Kodak Teen-Age Movie Contest, Eastman Kodak Company, Rochester, New York. The 1966 winner was a fourteen-year-old who produced a fifteen-minute 8mm film entitled "The Trip." It was the story about a young boy who takes the drug LSD. The film records (in black and white and color) the boy's hallucinations and ultimate terrible torments. The young boy who won this award said, "I learned by doing and reading photography magazines. I had no professional help."

Make a film—a film "with a mind of its own."

STUDYING AND WORKING WITH THE FILM

Mr. James Wicklund, chairman of the Communication Arts and Skills Department, Notre Dame High School, Niles, Illinois, has stated regarding the film curriculum at his high school, "There is perhaps no more influential literature today than film. We feel very much committed to the transition of society from verbal to visual concepts."

Such a statement from a leader in the field of education seems to indicate that churches studying and working with the film are participants in a new form of communicating truths about God and about man and the human situation. For this reason the programming and setting-up of a film study, be it a series of films or a single film, require prepara-

tion. Preparation is required in terms of the physical setting, the leader's competence, and the concern for those viewing and participating in reaction to the film.

It is important to remember that the viewers, *the people,* are the key to a good film session—people who are free to share, talk, and relate. Films communicate clearly to most people, especially young people. Thus the leader ought to respect the dignity and integrity of each person and allow the viewers the full potential for honest, open discussion, accepting differing viewpoints and convictions.

PREPARATION

1. Selecting the film

At the conclusion of this section is a listing of films, film guides, and film libraries. A post card to any of the commercial film libraries requesting a catalog will bring immediate response. Visit your local public library and check their film list. Often the public library will have the films you want and will provide them free of charge.

Film reviews of major films may be clipped from magazines and newspapers for future reference. In reading film reviews remember that each reviewer has his own personal criteria for review, and therefore a good film sometimes may receive a bad review. Read several reviews of a film to capture a wider perspective of the film. *The New Yorker, Saturday Review of Literature, Esquire,* and the *New York Times* offer excellent reviews. The "Film Guide" section toward the end of this chapter offers several resources for reviews of feature and shorter films.

In selecting a film know your group and know your theme in order that the film may be used to the best advantage.

2. Financing the Film

Rental prices for films vary greatly. The shorter films may range from $7.50 to $30.00. Feature length films may range from $25.00 to $100.00. Most films are rented for *one* showing and the rental agency will request an additional fee if the film is shown twice. Many commercial film companies will demand a higher rental fee if the film is shown where admission is charged to the public.

Financing the film may be shared in a church by the church budget; Sunday School or Day School treasury; men's, women's, or youth group contributions; or personal gifts.

3. Time for Viewing

The shorter films (five to thirty minutes) may be shown at almost any time from Sunday mornings to group meetings during the week. The feature length film requires more time, particularly when discussion is to follow. It is advisable to discuss a film immediately after a showing rather than to wait even a few hours.

Television is a valuable resource for viewing films. A group may arrange to discuss a particular film by viewing it on television in a home or at church. This has the advantage of film viewing without cost.

The local movie theater is often willing to arrange group rates for any group which desires to see a particular film. Discussion can follow the viewing at a local restaurant or in a private home.

4. The Setting

The obvious necessities for showing a film are often neglected, such as providing a projector operator who can handle any emergency; providing a large enough screen for the film and a dark room for the viewing; seeing that enough chairs are available and good air circulation is taking place; providing extra fuses and bulbs for the projector.

5. Preview the Film

It is important to preview the film. In the preview session the leader should note scenes, actions, situations, symbols, etc., which offer insights for understanding and interpreting the film. He should also serve as a resource person during the discussion.

Many of the shorter films may be previewed several times. Care should be exercised against prejudging a film.

Often young people are able to perceive the depth of a film before adults because of natural language problems which separate them. Beware of thinking, "I don't understand the film, therefore the youth will not understand it," or "This may be offensive to my group." You may be placing an unfair judgment upon yourself and the group. You can trust the young people and the power of God to move them to honest reaction.

DISCUSSING THE FILM

A film may "stand" by itself. It can be an end in itself, a valid art form which needs no discussion by its viewers. However, growth and stimulation come as people begin to interact and relate to one another. The mutual viewing of a film can become a catalyst for a group of people to say something significant to one another about themselves, their

A scene from "Lord of the Flies"

faith, and their stance in life, particularly as it relates to the life and action of the film viewed.

Freedom is important to good film discussion. It is the discussion leader's job to assure an open give-and-take. He is to guide the discussion but not force dogmatic views. He may ask pointed questions to get the discussion going, and after that he must respect the opinion of others and not react immediately to what he might judge a "false" interpretation. Any good film discussion must reserve quick judgments relating to the story of characters. The leader should help the group dig deep for understanding of the position of each character and how his role in the film contributes to the story itself. Specific behavior ought not be judged until situations are known and understood.

The following guides are only sample discussion outlines. A leader may combine these samples or create his own format for discussion.

Discussion Sample I

Upon viewing a film present the following four questions to the gathered group. Divide into smaller groups in order to discuss the questions. When groups return have each group share their comments and then have a general discussion by all present.

1. What emotions and specific ideas did you see operating in the talk and/or behavior of the people? (hysteria, love, hate, suspicion, etc.)

2. What effects did these thoughts and emotions have on the characters? (fighting, repentance, discovery of self, confession, reprisal, etc.)

3. What social structures and rules were present? (the social values and laws of the particular society, loss of face, role of women, etc.)

4. What social values were prominent from the interaction of the people?

(how did the social laws and values of their society touch the people involved, etc.)

The task of this discussion is to understand the setting in which the story of the film takes place. It is important to accept the story and people in terms of *their* society. This will enable the discussants to take the story seriously and avoid prejudgments.

Once the setting has been established we may ask further questions, such as:

1. What is the Christian's role in any of the situations presented?

2. Does the film speak to the Christian in today's situation? How?

3. Does the film say anything of the church's role in the world?

Discussion Sample II

When introducing a film say very little. Let the film be free to do its work without precast bias. The leader may simply show the film with no prior comments and let the anticipation build up while the group is viewing the film. The following lead questions may precipitate meaningful discussion in a large group setting:

1. What portion of the film impressed you?

2. What minor/major role impressed you?

3. Were there any particularly disturbing scenes?

4. Was there a character you liked/disliked?

5. Was there a scene in the film which might have indicated where God was involved?

6. Was there a situation or character which displayed Christ's kind of love?

7. In what way did the film or a character in the film say something to or about us as the "people of God"?

8. Did the film reveal anything of the church's role in the community? Its purpose? Its effectiveness?

Most often there are no simple answers or questions in dramatic situations. Many times an individual must struggle for an answer. Beware of easy "right" answers because the "right" answer may be wrong in some situations.

°**Discussion Sample III**

The *Dialog With the World* film program offers the following discussion format for feature films. The format will vary with shorter, documentary type films.

A. Questions to help participants remember all of the film and not just the last part or the climactic parts:

1. Which scene do you recall most vividly?

2. Which inanimate objects do you recall?

3. Which music?

4. Which minor character do you remember strongly?

5. Which room or setting?

6. Which love scene?

7. Were you conscious of sounds?

(*By the time these questions have circulated the entire group a few times almost the entire picture has been recalled and eagerness to participate sharpened. The whole film is now "present" to the minds of those in the discussion group.*)

B. Questions that help the people clarify their subjective reactions to the characters and situations:

1. Do you recall your own moods while watching?

2. Do you recall any moments when you or the group laughed nervously?

3. To which character were you drawn, at what time in the film? Did you change your viewpoint?

4. By what character were you repelled, at what time in the film? Did you change?

°*This discussion guide used with permission of Films Incorporated, a subsidiary of Encyclopedia Britannica Films, Inc.*

5. Were you ever angry with any of the characters? Why?

6. Did you ever feel uneasy with any of them? When?

C. Questions that bring to bear the language-symbols traditional to the Christian faith, but now in a life-interpreted way:

1. Where was rebellion against God (sin) evident in the film?

2. Was there a scene which showed people in the midst of change, becoming new people? (Can this be related to baptism, daily dying and rising, death and resurrection?)

3. Was there evident in the film a situation or character which displayed the kind of love Christ has for man? (The love which offers itself freely at the risk of death or abuse.)

4. Where in the film would it have been possible to display our commitment of mission and service?

It is important to remember that a film may not have been designed for a religious slant, but if the film is speaking about people in human situations, we can speak of the times and situations where God may have been moving or where we could have been free to bring the Gospel.

Discussion Sample IV

Each of the prior discussion suggestions may be combined with the following discussion starters:

1. Was the title of the film well chosen? Did the title relate to the theme of the film or was it chosen for another reason?

2. Do you recognize the name of the director of the film? Can you recall other films directed by this person? If so, do his other films have similarities to this film?

3. Do you think the film offered honest portrayal of the story or theme? Would you have made any changes in the film?

4. What did the film encourage in

terms of morality, values, faith, family, school, personal relationships, etc.?

Sample Discussion for the Short Film "Parable"

(The film *Parable*, discussed earlier in this section on films, may be ordered from most church film departments, both regional and local. If one particular church body does not have the film on hand, call another denominational office in your area.)

1. What is the most vivid scene that you remember from the movie?

2. Do you remember any of the music?

3. Do you recall any particular sounds?

4. Who was the clown (mime)? Did it seem to you that he was the Christ? Could he be any Christian? Why? Why not?

a. Did it disturb him that not everyone was his friend?

b. How did he make enemies?

c. Does it disturb you when people react negatively to you even though you seem not to deserve it?

5. Did it bother you that the central character was a clown or pantomimist? Why?

a. Would it have been better if the central character had been a carpenter, a logger, a clothing salesman, an actress, a teacher, a writer, a lawyer, a secretary, a farmer, a street sweeper?

b. Would it really have made any difference what his occupation was? Why? Why not?

6. What did it mean to you when:

a. The clown dusted with the broom in front of the children?

b. Magnus pulled the strings of the marionettes?

c. The clown appeared, following the parade at the end of the picture?

d. The group was seated together by the roadside as the parade went by?

e. Magnus applied the white make-up at the close of the story?

FILMS

The following are some of the films which have been used in church settings and received favorable reviews. The recommendation of a film does not imply blanket endorsement of every idea, portrayal, dialog, or conclusion of the film. Each person will react differently to a film. Young people generally are more receptive to a film than are adults simply because they have been raised with films and television.

Parentheses following title indicate length of film, rental fee (subject to change), and rental source (see Film Libraries list below).

Very Nice, Very Nice (8 minutes—$10.00—Contemporary). A powerful film which presents commentary on our day as the world might look through the eyes of someone young and uncommitted.

Two Men and a Wardrobe (15 minutes—$25.00—Contemporary). An eloquent fantasy-parable about the value of humans in our modern world.

Living (Vivre) (15 minutes—$7.00—Contemporary). The shock and impression left behind by war is told through the faces of the "family of man."

An Occurrence at Owl Creek Bridge (27 minutes—$17.50—Contemporary). An excellent drama dealing with the impending death of a man and his desire to live.

Adventures of ° (10 minutes—$10.00—Contemporary). The growth of man from the creative days of childhood to the humdrum of everyday life. Excellent.

Neighbors (9 minutes—$5.00—Contemporary). An allegorical study of two neighbors and what can happen when greed and hate comes to them.

Christmas in Appalachia (29 minutes—$10.00—Mass Media Ministries). The stark poverty and hopelessness of one million persons living in the desolation of Appalachia. May be shown at any season of the year.

No Reason to Stay (27 minutes—$8.00—Contemporary). Sensitive film related to the problems of education and drop-outs. Avoids the usual stereotypes and clichés frequently found in "drop-out" films.

The Game (27 minutes—$8.00—Contemporary). Excellent film dealing with young people, sex, and the meaning of relationships.

(Additional suggestions are offered in the *Arts Festival* section of this book under the sample of an arts festival film program.)

FILM GUIDES

Mass Media Ministries. A bi-weekly bulletin offering up-to-date film reviews, television programs, record notes, and radio programming. An excellent guide for a church's encounter with the arts. Address: Mass Media Ministries, 2116 North Charles Street, Baltimore, Maryland 21218.

Saint Clement's Film Association. A monthly bulletin offering film and television reviews and discussion guides. Address: The Saint Clement's Film Association, 423 West 46th Street, New York, New York 10036.

Catholic Film Newsletter. An excellent bimonthly guide offering reviews of current films as well as information regarding the film industry. Address: Catholic Film Newsletter, 453 Madison Avenue, New York, New York 10022.

The Green Sheet. Lists current and forthcoming films. Address: Film Estimate Board of National Organizations, 28 West 44th Street, New York, New York 10036.

Scholastic Roto. A high school magazine which contains film reviews as well as articles related to young people and films. Conducts contest each year for best film reviews written by young people for a communication media. Available in most high schools. Address: National Scholastic Press Association, 41 East 42nd Street, New York, New York 10017.

Media and Methods. A journal for high school educators but containing useful information for the church about the use of various media in education. Address: Media and Methods, 124 East 40th Street, New York, New York 10016.

Dialog With the World—Offers a program of feature length films with study guides. Write for free brochure. Among the more than 100 films available with study guides are *Becket, Edge of the City, Citizen Kane, On the Waterfront, Hud,* and *All About Eve.* Write to: "Films Incorporated" for information related to *Dialog With the World.* See library listing for "Films Incorporated" office in your area.

Films for Religious Education. A paperback book offering ratings and reviews of many films suitable for church use. Cost is $1.00. Address: Fides Publishers, Inc., Notre Dame, Indiana.

Short Films in Religious Education. William Kuhns, Pflaum Publishers, Dayton, Ohio ($7.50)

Children and the Light. A guide to short films for church use. Cost is 75c. Address: St. Mary of the Lake Seminary, Mundelein, Illinois.

(Due to constant changing costs, the subscription rates of the above are not listed. "The Green Sheet" is available free of charge.)

FILM LIBRARIES

Most of the distributors listed have catalogs and brochures available upon request. Most church bodies have their own film distribution centers and are too numerous to mention. Possibly the richest source of films is the local public library. Many libraries are beginning to include films in their collections. Prior to ordering a film (notably the short subject) investigate its availability at your local library.

American Art and History Films (Films on art, poetry, experimental subjects), 41 West 47th Street, New York, New York 10036.

Anti-Defamation League (Films, mostly television productions), 315 Lexington Avenue, New York, New York 10016.

Audio Film Center (American and foreign feature films, Disney features, experimental short subjects):
Midwest—2138 East 75th Street, Chicago, Illinois 60649
East —200 West 57th Street, New York, New York 10019
West —Western Cinema Guild, 381 Bush Street, San Francisco, California 94104

Carousel Films, Inc. (Original television productions), 1501 Broadway, New York, New York 10036.

Cinema 16 (American and foreign experimental and art short subjects and features), 175 Lexington Avenue, New York, New York 10016.

Contemporary Films, Inc. (Short Subjects, documentaries, National Film Board of Canada films):
Midwest—828 Custer Avenue, Evanston, Illinois 60202
East —267 West 25th Street, New York, New York 10001
West —1211 Poly Street, San Francisco, California 96209

Creative Film Society (Creative short subjects by Eames, Hubley, McLaren, etc., and other unique experimental, documentary and abstract films), 14558 Valerio Street, Van Nuys, California 91405.

Films Incorporated (American feature films from major studios, Dialog With the World series, Encyclopedia Britannica short subjects):

Midwest—4420 Oakton Street, Skokie, Illinois 60076
26539 Grand River, Detroit, Michigan 48240
East —38 West 32nd Street, New York, New York 10001
West —2129 N.E. Broadway, Portland, Oregon 97232
5626 Hollywood Blvd., Hollywood, California 90028
South —277 Pharr Road, N.E., Atlanta, Georgia 30305
1414 Dragon Street, Dallas, Texas 75207

Institutional Cinema Service, Inc. (American and foreign feature films and short subjects)
Midwest—203 N. Wabash Avenue, Chicago, Illinois 60601
East —29 East 10th Street, New York, New York 10003

Janus Film Library (Ingmar Bergman films, Italian and French short subjects) 25 West 58th Street, New York, New York

Mass Media Ministries (Resource for many films for church use), 2116 North Charles Street, Baltimore, Maryland

Museum of Modern Art Film Library (American and foreign films from 1895 to the present) 11 West 53rd Street, New York, New York 10019

Rembrandt Film Library (Experimental films) 267 West 25th Street, New York, New York 10001

Trans-World Films (Feature films from France, Germany, Great Britain, Japan, Spain, Mexico, Sweden and the United States) 332 South Michigan Blvd., Chicago, Illinois 60604

Twyman Films, Inc. (Feature films from Universal, Columbia, Disney, UA,

Paramount, UPA, Rank. Exclusive distributors of von Sternberg films) 329 Salem Avenue, Dayton, Ohio 45401

United World Films (American and British films)
Midwest—542 Dearborn Street, Chicago, Illinois 60605
East —221 Park Avenue, New York, New York 10003
West —7374 Melrose Avenue, Los Angeles, California 90046
South —287 Techwood Drive, Atlanta, Georgia 30313

WBBM-TV Film Loan Library (Television documentaries and public affairs programs) 630 N. McClur Court, Chicago, Illinois 60611

FILM READING LIST

This list is compiled for those who desire to do research and study related to the use of the film.

Movies: Universal Language (film study in high school) Sister Bede Sullivan, O.S.B. Fides Publishers, Notre Dame, Indiana.

Film Study in the High School. John Culkin. Fordham Film Study Center, Fordham University, New York, New York.

Film World. Ivor Montagu. Penguin Books.

I Lost It at the Movies. Pauline Kael. Bantam Books.

Mass Communications and Education. Educational Policies Commission, National Education Association, 1206 16th Street, Washington, D.C.

Motion Pictures. A. R. Fulton. University of Oklahoma Press.

The Filmviewers Handbook. E. McAnay and R. Williams. Paulist Press.

The Liveliest Art. Arthur Knight. Signet Books.

The Screen Arts. Edward Fischer. Sheed and Ward.

The Good News And The Daily News

"The newspaper of the future," asserts Wall Street Journal president Bernard Kilgore, "must become an instrument of intellectual leadership, an institution of intellectual development—a center of learning."

(*Newsweek*, November 29, 1965)

We have at our fingertips two forms of the printed word. They reveal and expose the condition of man and the action of God in the world and in our community. These are the Holy Scriptures (Good News) and the newspaper (daily news). Each of these speaks of a style of living.

In the Good News we discover God working through the ordinary affairs of man. His Son takes on human form. The common elements of water, bread and wine, together with words (proclamation, confession, absolution), are ways God uses to invade our daily lives. In the Good News we have the record of God working in historical events, using the lives of men and the actions of a people to reveal himself.

The daily news offers a record of man's history in the present. In its various forms (newspaper, *Time, Newsweek,* etc.) it floods our homes, schools, newsstands, and offices, carrying tragic stories of napalm bombs, murder on the highway, divorce cases, suicide and poverty, theft and rape, as well as the obituary column, that constant reminder of *our* "making" the news. The daily news reports man's situation in the present. It tells of people struggling to gain freedom in the midst of hate and poverty, new and exciting scientific advances, and good samaritans offering their lives for others.

At the same time the daily news offers an occasion for faith to see the power of sin in man's life, and the judgment and concern of God. In the life cycle of the daily news the arena for Christian witness and love is described. It suggests how we can come to grips with some of the "gut-action" required of the Christian in the world.

The daily news, when studied with the Scriptures, opens our eyes to the meaning of life in the world in terms of our Christian commitment. The newspaper gears us to the *present* direction of the world and indicates those areas where our Christian concern and commitment must be worked out in service to the world.

WHAT IS THE NEWS?

In its purest sense the information offered in the newspaper is that news which the editor feels will interest the reader. News is true when the facts are given. A departure from these facts is "editorializing," that is, offering and adding the personal view of the editor or the philosophy of the local newspaper. In different newspapers the same story will be handled in different ways.

News has the quality of *nowness* about it. Something has just happened. What is it? What is the relationship of this news to me, to my neighbor?

Since many people enjoy the sensational, the frequent element of the unusual in the news makes newspapers sell. Some read newspapers for "totem" purposes, choosing a paper which supports their own personal viewpoint: they know the stand the newspaper will always take on an issue and read it because they know it will help bolster their private position. At the same time, others with a concern for the world about them read the newspaper for information and stimulation. In any case, the newspaper takes on an added meaning for the Christian when he is a sensitive servant in the world.

A LOOK AT THE NEWSPAPER

The daily newspaper calls the Christian to respond to his world. One form of response may be an act of *judgment*. He may be forced to question the way an item of news was reported, the "slant" given it by the paper, or the event itself about which he read in the daily news as a "prophet" of God. He may also be called to *act*, that is, to place himself and God's concern in the midst of some human event. The Christian cannot be divorced from the action and life of the world and must view some human events as challenges to personal involvement and action.

The reaction of judgment or action may come in response to four general areas which compose the content of the newspaper:

The *Political News* both at home and abroad will offer evidence of the course of certain events which take place in our world. In viewing the political scene of the world the Christian can observe God using all kinds of people to do his will.

Human Events make up much of the content of the daily newspaper. It is these events which touch us most closely. Shouts of joy and cries of help are to be found in each edition. Such mixtures of sorrow and happiness seek the action and involvement of the Christian.

Editorial Comment assists in shaping the mind of the readers for good or bad. Many opinions are formed in individuals and groups through this section of the news. The discussion of such opinions from a base of intelligence and information will enable a reader to bring truth to a situation which often carries half-truths or personal views as the truth.

Entertainment and the Arts are the sections of the newspaper in which sensitive artists attempt to tell the world something about itself. Art exhibitions, films, drama, etc., assist the Christian toward a view of the world in which he

34

finds himself. In a sense this view sets the agenda for the Christian response in the world.

LISTEN TO THE NEWSPAPER

The Christian not only reads but also "listens" to the message of God as it comes through the daily news. Instead of being at the mercy of the stance of a particular newspaper, the Christian attempts to have a clear-eyed view of the world which surrounds him, using the daily news as a vehicle of revelation in the present world.

Many people wisely read two or three newspapers each day in order to grasp a fuller perspective on a given issue and thereby define the issue for themselves on the basis of good solid thinking from opposing views. Such a procedure might well commend itself to Christians who ought to be accurately informed for their life in God's world.

USING THE DAILY NEWS

1. As you study the Scriptures use the daily newspaper (as well as *Time, Newsweek, Life,* school papers, etc.) to highlight similar life situations faced by the leaders and prophets of the Old Testament and the church of today. What is the church's response in terms of Jesus Christ, Lord of *all,* to newspaper items such as:

a. "Ann Landers" type columns

b. Editorials

c. National and local affairs (politics, welfare, education, taxes, imports, automation, civil rights, etc.)

d. The advertisements (and state laws) which deal with loan company advertisements. Is usury involved? Does the state law make high interest repayments "right" in the eyes of the Christian?

2. What style of living does your local newspaper portray? Is there a response to this message? How does the news portray the power of the demonic in the world? Is the lordship of Jesus Christ present in the news reports?

3. Newspapers are geared to reporting the facts. Does your newspaper perform this task? Are the reports slanted in favor of a particular group in your community or a certain point of view (does the paper report from a Republican or Democratic political stance, etc.)? What does it mean to read a newspaper "with discernment"?

4. The newspaper serves as a potential worship resource. Traditional pleas and petitions of the church can be symbolized by reading portions of the newspaper as the versicle. For example, an obituary heading can be read, followed by the response, "Lord, have

mercy." A prayer litany can be developed using this method. A prayer petition for the hungry of the world can be summed up by reading a paragraph of a hunger report from India. Reports in the newspaper can also reflect the goodness of God and be used as a doxology.

5. Invite the editor of your local newspaper to your group for a discussion on such topics as:

a. Why are "minors" not mentioned by name in "lead" news stories?

b. Do local papers have agreements not to print certain news? Why? Good or bad?

c. What is "managed" news?

d. How do "news services" affect local coverage?

e. How are photographs selected and used to report news stories?

f. You might also discuss the following areas: (1) newspaper dealings and reportings with labor and management; (2) style of advertising [how is advertising selected, and what controls relating to selection of advertising does the paper use]; (3) how does the paper select and train reporters, editors, photographers; (4) what is the role of the newspaper besides reporting the news; (5) can news be reported objectively; and (6) what is the relationship between the newspaper's stand on obscene literature and its own printing of "suggestive" pictures in film advertisements in the movie guide pages?

6. Conduct a study, having the Bible in one hand and the newspaper in the other. Interpret each in light of the other. In what way is the Bible *daily news* as well as Good News? In what way is the newspaper *Good News* as well as daily news? (Example: Compare the Exodus of Israel with the civil rights movement. Are there similarities? Are there differences? Is it legitimate to study each in the light of the other?)

7. Use the newspaper (and magazines) to make a collage. (A collage [ko-lázh] is an assemblage of pictures and words cut from the newspaper which express a feeling, mood, view, worship, etc.) Ask the youth to design their own collage relating to the following subjects:

Youth's view of the church

Youth's view of their parents

Youth's view of the world

Youth's view of their youth group

. . . and many more.

At the same time you may design a collage relating to your view of the youth culture. The ensuing discussion relating to the designs will aid you in your understanding of youth as they view life through the eyes and ears of a collage. Try it!

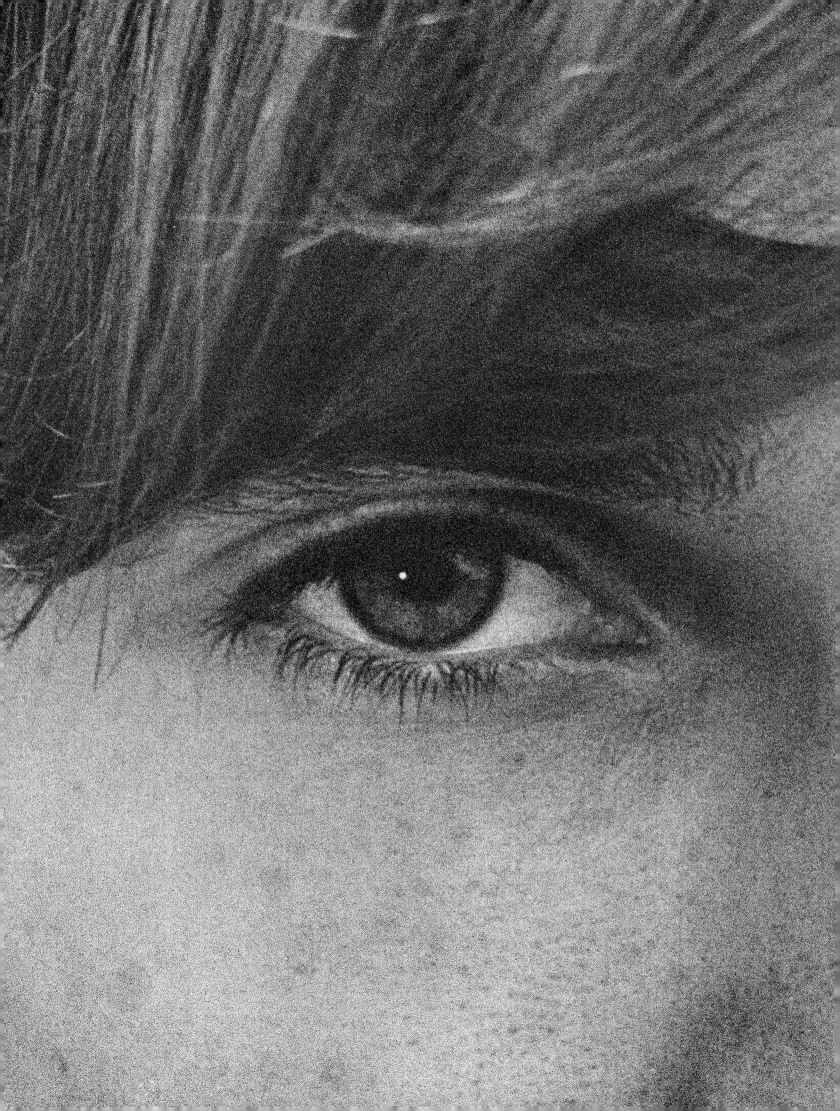

Pop
Goes
The
Music

"The New Youth is finding its poets on juke boxes and its religion in rock 'n roll, its preachers in night clubs, and its philosophers with long hair and guitars. They are bound to come into conflict with authority, just as every religious movement has."

(The Great War Between Kids and Society, *Ralph Gleason*)

For the first time in history music is being written by and for young people. The youth of America (and the world) are writing and singing their own songs. They own record companies and are creating their own market for music. Youthful music, offering defiant, free, and odd sounds, is being purchased by the young. And the music keeps coming! Youthful impact in the music world has resulted in youth's "owning" one form of mass media for the first time in history —the radio. Stations throughout the United States are designed for the specific purpose of meeting and molding the minds of young people.

MUSIC AND HISTORY

Many authorities insist that music is a reflection of social history, that the kind of music which is popular at a given time is that which reflects the mood, attitudes, and feelings which are prevalent in that society.

The music of our post-World War II era might tend to validate such a theory. The Tin Pan Alley tunes of the pre-war and immediate post-war periods were designed to amuse and add a decorative aspect to people's lives. Many of the tunes were "escapist," designed for generations caught in an isolationist ghetto. After the war the nation was caught up in a sensational mood; the lights were going on around the world. The names of Frank Sinatra, Perry Como, and Andy Russel dominated the music market with such songs as "Prisoner of Love," "Unchained," and "To Each His Own." Three or four leading singers dominated the record industry, which was composed of five major recording companies. Many of the songs of this period remained at the top of the Hit Parade for weeks, filling the airwaves and selling a million records per tune over a period of months.

The times have changed and so has the music! This is an age of noise. Jets zoom over communities, filling the air with sonic booms. Television floods the home with sound as youngsters watch their favorite programs, and the ears of a new generation are glued to transistor radios. It is an age of conflict, with blood being spilled in Selma, Watts, Newark, Detroit, and Viet Nam. It is an age of courage, seen in the faces of the seekers of justice. It is an age of movements, with civil rights activities capturing the spirit of many young people, and the far right and far left attempting to influence the mind of the adolescent. It is an age of discovery, the invention of laser beams and accomplishment of moon landings. It is an age of money—before you have read half of this page young people in the United States will have spent $2,378.22. It is an age which displays its delinquency, drug addiction, and sexual promiscuity. It is the age of the "jerk" and the "frug" and the New Sentimentality; an age of new forms, new cultural patterns, new ideas, and new conformity. It is an age in which all share the common attribute of sin and have the opportunity for a refreshed life in Jesus Christ. It is an age when many of the noises, discoveries, and excitement are recognized by Christian people as gifts of God and evidence of his ongoing creation.

In the midst of this age, the 60's, *Pop Goes the Music.* The "Sound of the Sixties" is not the same as that of the 40's. On any week you may find seven to ten personalities in the "Top 10." Each of these personalities may have sold one million of their records in one month or less. The songs will remain a top hit for perhaps one to three weeks. Record companies have multiplied many times and it is possible to see seven or eight different record companies listed in the "Top 10" each week, and many more in the "Top 40."

SOUNDS OF POP MUSIC

Time in its article on Rock 'n Roll (May 21, 1965, pp. 84-86, 88) called the Big Beat music of the teen world the "Sound of the Sixties." For some ten years there have been predictions that the big sound, the beat, would suffer the fate of other fads of music and die; but the Sound of the Sixties is very much alive. "It has become, in fact," comments the *Time* article, "the international anthem of a new and restless generation, the pulse beat for new modes of dress, dance, language, art and morality."

Pop music resembles the diversity of the sixties. One can no longer type the "Top 40" (the replacement of the Hit Parade and Tin Pan Alley) as containing a single type of message or mode. At any given time the following are likely to be listed in the top tunes of the week: country, folk, rhythm, and blues, gospel, jazz, folk-rock, and love songs. None of these categories will dominate the "Top 40" for any length of time.

Accompanying the Big Beat is the Big Noise, the advent of the electronic guitar. During the one year of 1965

Music

one-third of all musical instruments sold in the United States were electronic guitars. It is estimated that seven million Americans now strum a guitar, many of them electronic. Pete Seeger, called the "father of the modern-day folk music movement" and noted guitarist, has said, "The electronic guitar might prove to be the most typical folk instrument of the 21st century."

The rise of the guitar, particularly the electronic guitar, has created a generation of musicians. Young people are forming musical combos and writing music as never before. Many adults may not realize that of the hundreds of tunes being recorded each month most are written by young people.

A high school newspaper, interviewing a number of the musical combos in its school newspaper, received the following response from the young musicians: "We enjoy making music"; "we are doing something worthwhile for others"; "it's fun"; "performing gives you pride and that pride makes you do other things better, including homework." A teacher stated, "The whole level of musicianship has greatly improved." The same newspaper also reported that the amount of money spent for equipment by these groups ranged from $2,000 to $5,000. These groups have adopted such names as The End of Times, The Lonely Souls, The Rising Tides, The Abstractions, and The Last Words.

THE MUSIC

The music of the younger generation may be classified in three general categories:

Folk music has as its source messages of protest and joy. Folk tunes generally have a "biting edge" to them and often find difficulty in being accepted by an older generation. A folk singer will be accepted by a younger group, for the music comes through to them unabashed, reflecting the life and times in which the youth live.

Folk-Rock is folk music with a "big beat." Folk-Rock draws upon folk material and converts it for popular consumption. A leader in the "conversion" has been Bobby Dylan. Dylan began his musical career and received fame as a folk singer. He then adapted his music and lyrics for the big beat and became a folk-rock musician.

Rock is the big beat, using a driving rhythm accompanied by electronic guitars, organs, and drums. It is the most popular of youthful music.

THE SOUND

The creation and performance of Pop Music is in the hands of a young, amateur generation developing new exciting sounds and comments for the world. Much of the music is simple and accessible to all. The music speaks of God, love, hate, war, and freedom. It is providing youthful heroes for a youth generation, a generation which doesn't simply want to get educated, go to war, have kids, and die—a generation which desires to live and is struggling to find the way. Such a generation creates music which displays sensitivity to people and the action of the world around us. A young thinking and writing generation is writing for the people of their age.

This young generation has made their music a cultural heritage. One need not like all of it any more than one needs to like all of the "classics." Perhaps only five to ten percent of the present music can be considered good to excellent; yet, it is an improvement over the music of past generations because it expresses the kinetic needs and emotional attitudes of young people in a more authentic fashion.

The Beatles' music, for example, is as inventive and exciting as any that could be found. And though the Beatles are passing into history their music will remain, for "beatle-like" music is much closer to Bach's and Mozart's exciting style than most people seem to realize.

The "Top 40" is a good thing. Its forty top-selling records bring pleasure, joy, and frequent identity. If music is a catalyst, then the "Top 40" offers the opportunity for expressions of joy, sorrow, dancing, and commentary. Diversity in life is a gift of God, a heritage of our country, a strength to the individual, and Pop Music offers diversity for the young.

An older generation finds it difficult to understand the cultural forms and language of the younger generation. In defense of a portion of the "generation gap" it must be said that adults have as much right to reject these new forms of music as do the youth to reject the older adult forms. The problem lies not so much in forcing mutual acceptance of forms as it does in arriving at mutual understanding of the forms and the people who use them. What we must realize is that "adults will be adults" and "youth will be youth," and soon the sounds of the sixties will be rejected by the sounds of the seventies. This does not minimize today's sound and its life pattern for this generation.

Adults in the church ought to recognize that this music is a valid part of the teen-ager's life, and that it is not the task of the church to condemn such music but rather to enable Christian young people to be perceptive to its message and trust in their judgmental powers. "Young people," observes Pete Seeger, "will ridicule and ignore hack tunes, and will continue to sing the occasional good ones." Talking about hack tunes and good tunes with young people will enable the church to minister to and enjoy its young people; it will enable Christian young people to perceive the influence of music in their lives and to use their perception to influence the new age of the world.

WORKING WITH POP MUSIC

(Tunes change, so it is difficult to take specific examples of songs for this study. A tune mentioned here will not be popular when the reader digs into this presentation. Hopefully the reader will adapt the study suggestions to the "Top 40" of his day.)

POP MUSIC GROUP

Form a Pop Music Group in your congregation. The purpose: (a) to discover what makes the pop music world tick; (b) to equip youth to become sensitive to the influence of that world on their Christian morals and values; (c) to discuss the sounds and lyrics of the Big Beat in the light of Christian concerns for boy-girl relationships, for social and political concerns, for concerns related to the Christian understanding of life and death, for talking about meaning and purpose in this world in terms of the lyrics; and (d) to enjoy the more creative, wholesome offerings of the Pop Music world.

1. Study

   a. Hold record sessions. Ask each member to bring his favorite albums or 45's.

   b. Talk about the lyrics of the tunes represented. What is their message or tack? Any reflection on our Christian faith in the lyrics? What do you recognize about yourself in the song?

   c. Have the group read portions of *The World of Pop Music and Jazz* by William Robert Miller. React to the comments in this book related to Pop Music. (See reading list.)

2. Encounter

   a. Have the group attend a local DJ show. If possible make arrangements to speak to the DJ.

   b. Visit a local recording company. Speak to the executives about the history and marketing of Pop Music. Who writes the lyrics of the songs? What group buys records? How is a record "pushed"?

   c. The counselors can attend a local record hop or school dance to view the young people in action with their music. Talk to the school counselor regarding the influence of music and his reaction to the music and impact of the dance.

   d. As a group, view a television session which features Pop Music "in action."

3. Action

   a. Discuss reactions to the encounter phase of the study.

   b. Invite a DJ to your session and discuss with him Pop Music and your reactions to the encountered situations.

   c. Based on your prior study, reflect on these questions: Why can Pop Music artists be successful by pushing tunes that talk about loneliness? death? What's good about Pop Music? What directions do the lyrics give to young people? What are the words really saying?

   d. Trace the source of the Pop Music tune under study. Is it gospel-tune oriented or folk, folk-rock, country, jazz, blues? Do the protest songs speak to our age? Which protest songs are honest? phony?

   e. Attempt to observe which type of songs "click" by gathering "Top 40" song lists from the local record shop. Keep a file on the "Top 40" over a period of several weeks. Which songs appear to be in style at the present time? Any changes in direction?

   f. Using an informal worship session, the group may wish to experiment by using pop tunes in the worship setting. A wise selection of contemporary music may find a meaningful place in informal, non-liturgical worship. Some groups have used the folk tune "Blowing in the Wind" as part of worship under the theme of a suffering and struggling church in the midst of the world. Another group sang "If I Had a Hammer" as an introduction to a mission-slanted worship setting.

READING LIST

The World of Pop Music and Jazz, William Robert Miller. Concordia Publishing House, St. Louis. Christian Encounter Series ($1.00).

Anything Goes: The World of Popular Music, David Dachs. Bobbs-Merrill, Indianapolis, Indiana.

Songs for Today, Ewald Bash, Concordia Publishing House, St. Louis.

Schwann Long Playing Record Catalog, W. Schwann, Inc., 137 Newbury Street, Boston, Massachusetts 02116 (A catalog published monthly containing lists of LP records available from all record companies. Available in most record shops. 40c.)

Educational Record Sales, 157 Chambers Street, New York, New York 10007.

(Write for catalog. Offers recordings for music, drama, and poetry for high school youth.)

OF INTEREST TO CHURCHES

A word needs to be said about the use of other records. In addition to the world of Pop Music, recently some interesting recordings have been produced related to the church. These records offer a variety of experiences for the youth of the church. The music and record explosion in our society has freed the church to celebrate with new forms of worship, song and prayer. A Pop Music group, or a general youth group meeting, might listen to these records and react out of their experience in both the pop world and the liturgical world of the church. Try some or all of the following:

Missa Bantu. Phillips Record (PCC211).

Missa Criolla. Phillips Record (PCC619).

The Easter Story. (Request study guide.) Act IV Productions, 3535 West Roosevelt Road, Chicago, Illinois.

Don't Cut the Baby in Half. 12805 B, 13th Avenue N., Minneapolis, Minnesota.

Allelu. FEL Records, Chicago, Illinois.

Missa Bossa Nova. FEL Records, Chicago, Illinois.

20 Century Folk Mass. Fiesta Record Company, 1619 Broadway, New York, New York. (FLP 25000) (Show-tune style).

Missa Luba. Phillips Record (PCC206) (African orientation).

Father River's American Mass Program. World Library of Sacred Music, 1846 Westwood Avenue, Cincinnati, Ohio (SP1002).

The American Folk Mass Program. North American Recording Company, Chicago, Illinois 60615 (CM6806) (Folk style).

Vince Guaraldi at Grace Cathedral. Fantasy Records (3367) (Jazz).

Jass Suite on Mass Texts. RCA Victor (LPM3414) (Sophisticated jazz).

Rejoice. Scepter Records, 254 West 54th Street, New York, New York (S527) (Folk style).

Are You Running With Me, Jesus. Columbia (CL2548) (Prayers by Malcolm Boyd).

Happening Prayers for Now. Columbia (CL2657) (Prayers by Malcolm Boyd).

Wait a Minute, Moses. Radio Station KFUO, St. Louis, Missouri (Exodus updated).

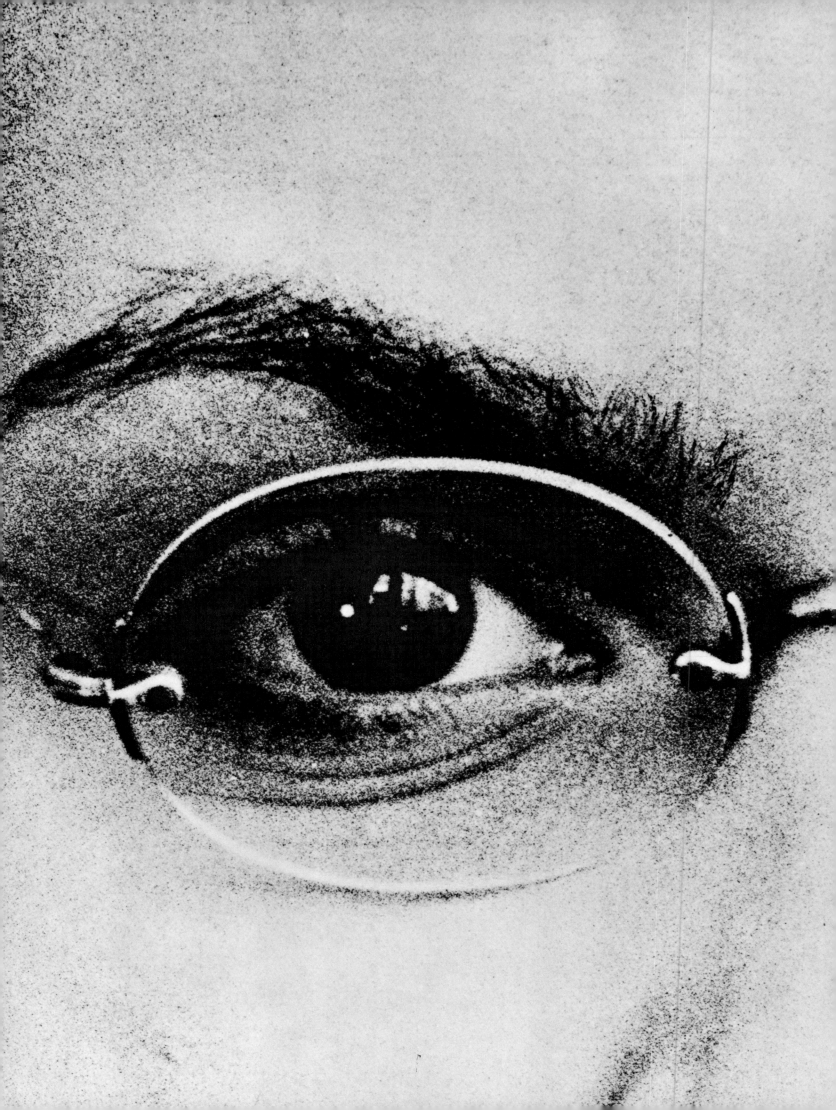

The Printed Page

" . . . for the printed book simply does not enter into the out-of-school-life of a subspecies of the modern adolescent. Anything that does not reach him by TV, radio, film, or the pages of a few popular newspapers, does not reach him, period."

(John Wain, *New Republic*)

There is a revolution taking place in the publishing industry. Most reports indicate that more people are reading books and enjoying it more. Books, like movies, are better than ever. *Publishers' Weekly,* the book industry journal, reports a great increase in book publishing. But at the same time this journal reports that even though people are reading and more books are being published, the reading habits of people are not keeping up with the population. Thus we are experiencing the paradox of more books and more readings, but a decline in the overall percentage of the population who buy books and enjoy them.

In recent years significant gains in publishing have been made in the fields of literature, music, philosophy, religion, and sports and recreation. New editions (paperbacks) are on the rise in the "juvenile" (youth) division. More and more publishing companies are responding to the paperback trend as well as the increase in "juvenile" publishing.

The advent of paperback books now makes it possible to acquire low cost books for group study and offers the advantage of building an adequate library for future reference at reasonably low cost. The publishing industry offers two listings for its paperbacks. The first, the "mass market paperbacks," are for general consumption. It includes books like *Catcher in the Rye, The Man,* and *In Cold Blood.* The second listing is "trade paperbacks." These are books designed for educational purposes or presentations of various studies. Books on this list would include such titles as *The Gospel According to Peanuts* and *Honest to God.*

Young people are caught up in this reading revolution. Literature and English departments of the high schools are demanding that youth not only read the classics but also the works of contemporary authors. High schools seem to be moving away from anthologies (collected works) and requesting students to purchase paperbacks for their studies.

There still is a question whether youth do much private, out-of-the-classroom reading. Many authorities wonder about the reading habits of young people. The available evidence seems to indicate that youth generally will read the occasional book that "catches on" but that intense and sustained reading by young people is not very common.

Books offer the opportunity to mull over situations, problems, comments, and characters. In contrast to the viewing of films or television, where a group cannot turn back to repeat a section or review a situation, book study offers an opportunity for engagement in much greater depth. It also affords material for the technique of dramatization.

Young people are reading, and what they read influences them. It should be the church's responsibility to help young people interpret what they read so that they understand, evaluate, judge, perceive, and enjoy it. By studying the diagnosis which an author makes of his society they can discover where an expression of the Gospel is most needed.

STUDYING THE NOVEL

For those interested in talking about books and what makes books exciting reading, a literature group may be formed. This group should schedule meetings for book selection and discussion. In order to get the group started it would be well to discover what books young people are already reading for high school assignments as well as for leisure. If the group begins with a book most people are reading in school (contact the high school literature department) or for leisure (contact the school librarian, local book store, best seller lists), the young people are usually most willing to get started and it will not place an additional burden on their academic load.

Simple Study Guide

1. Select a book for study. Provide a copy of the book for each member of the group. The leader of the group should "plow" the book thoroughly beforehand.

2. Discuss the general theme of the book. What appears to be its underlying purpose? What is the single thread which seems to tie the book together?

3. Lay down the ground rules for discussion. Stick to the point of the book. Let the author speak to you. Quote from the book. If you disagree with a point of view of the author or the interpretation of the author's point of view by another member of your group, don't hesitate to say so. Perhaps you can lubricate throats with coke and pizza during the discussion.

4. How can the book aid/deter your life as a Christian? Does the book have something meaningful and relevant to say to you, to your group, to your congregation? If it doesn't have anything to say, why not?

Detailed Study Guide

1. Define group purpose. A smaller group within the literature group may want to examine issues involved in a novel, or an issue of the church or society, by using the novel as a basis for the discussion.

2. Formulate the questions. Focus questions which the group may explore toward achieving its purpose.

a. Which persons or events in the book appear to be familiar to most of the group? Known by most? Real to most?

b. How did the attitudes of the characters in the book originate?

c. Are there key words which give clues to the purpose or problem in the book?

d. Are there certain "action" steps to be taken prior to the group discussion? (For instance, if studying human relations it would be advantageous to know how your city council, real estate agents, and church feel regarding the issue.)

3. Analyze the book.

a. What is happening to the people or issues in the book?

b. Recognize the range of problems and situations in the book.

c. Recognize the limitations of the book.

4. The study group

a. Make copies available to all members of the group. Suggest that the group read the book at least twice, underlining key sections as they read. Normally, two weeks will be sufficient.

b. Explain the purpose of the discussion and how the book will be used to accomplish this purpose.

c. Role play sections of the book. Have different members of the group play the parts of the characters in the novel, adopting their character and attitude for a brief episode. Show how you think that character responded to, or how he would respond to, similar situations in your town, family, or church.

d. Stop the role play and let the group react to the role playing as well as the book.

e. List on a blackboard the issues which could be discussed. Select the key issues for discussion.

f. Plan the steps for the next session.

Special assignments might be shared among the group members.

g. Plan the next meeting.

A discussion of this type can be used for young people or adults. The discussion of the book itself may be limited to one session, with following sessions given to discussion of problem areas and scriptural implications.

Discussing Themes

Discussions related to books may center around themes. A comparison of readings may offer added insight into such themes as human relations or alienation. The following books may be used for such discussions:

1. HUMAN RELATIONS:

Peaceable Lane. Keith Wheeler. Signet.

A Raisin in the Sun. Lorraine Hansberry. Signet.

Go Tell It on the Mountain. James Baldwin. Signet.

2. ALIENATION:

Lord of the Flies. William Golding. Capricorn Books.

Heart of Darkness. Joseph Conrad. Signet Classic.

Interview Themes

Let an individual within the group take on the character of one of the key personalities of the book (Elmer Gantry in *Elmer Gantry*, Dick Gregory in *Nigger*, the president in *The Man*, etc.) and be interviewed by members of the group who act as radio and television newsmen. The "newscasters" would attempt to probe into the character's life and discover motives for his actions and living.

BIBLIOGRAPHY FOR BOOK STUDY

In selecting a book for study determine the reading habits of the young people. Reading lists vary in different parts of

the country. Gather a suggested list of books from the high school librarian or high school literature department.

The following listing was made from book lists of various public and parochial high school literature departments; the American Library Association, Chicago, Illinois (*Book Bait*, detailed notes on adult books popular with young people, and *A Basic Collection for High Schools*); "Between the Grimms and the 'Group,'" *Literature in American High Schools*, Cooperative Test Division, Educational Testing Service, Princeton, New Jersey.

Profiles in Courage, John F. Kennedy (Pocket Books).

Diary of a Young Girl, Anne Frank (Pocket Books).

Lord Jim, Joseph Conrad (Modern Library).

To Kill a Mockingbird, Harper Lee (Popular Library).

Lord of the Flies, William Golding (Capricorn).

The Ugly American, William Lederer and Eugene Burdick (Fawcett).

The Power and the Glory, Graham Greene (Viking Press).

On the Beach, Nevil Shute (New American Library).

An American Tragedy, Theodore Dreiser (Dell).

The Old Man and the Sea, Ernest Hemingway (Scribner, Students Edition).

Status Seekers, Vance Packard (Pocket Books).

Catcher in the Rye, J. D. Salinger (Bantam).

Death Be Not Proud, John Gunther (Perennial).

Periodicals for the Leader

Publishers' Weekly, 62 West 45th Street, New York, New York.

Saturday Review, 25 West 45th Street, New York, New York.

Book Listings

American Library Association, 50 East Huron Street, Chicago, Illinois 60611.

American Book Publishers Council, 58 West 40th Street, New York, New York.

POETRY

Poetry is probably the most personal type of writing to be found in any society. The artist who creates a poem shouts to the world his feelings about life, death, pain, beauty, joy, war, school, and God. The poem might be written in free verse, blank verse, or a host of other rhymic schemes.

One poet has described poetry as "the lub-dub rhythm of the heart." It helps people think in new, fresh ways about the things of this world. A word of poetry can often sum up many feelings and expressions, and a series of poetic words offer an engaging form of human expression. The discovery of the power packed into a brief expression is one of the joys of reading poetry, for the poet attempts to encompass depth and understanding with a few words and in those few words lie the dynamics of what is said.

The movement and form of the poem can express a sensitivity to the currents of our life. The rich poetic forms of the Scriptures attest to this fact. Often the poet, as an artist and as a viewer of the world scene, can lead us into insights related to our mode of living as well as our struggle for meaning and commitment in life.

The recent trends in poetry toward "actual language" with less emphasis upon precise strictures of meter and rhyme have engaged many young people in the art of writing poetry. High schools are beginning to "swim" with poetry as the young begin to see the infinite possibilities of this form of expression. They are writing poetry which excites us and/or woos us into observing new sights in the world in which we live. Young people are accepting and understanding poetry. Hopefully, poetry can serve as a medium of expression and communication for the youth of the church.

WORKING WITH POETRY

1. Form a poetry group and spend sessions studying and discussing the poetry of a particular writer. Attempt to understand the images the poet is communicating. How does the poet struggle to communicate life's meaning? Is there a Christian response to the message of the poet? Search the writings of poets like E. E. Cummings, T. S. Eliot, Robert Frost, Dylan Thomas, and John Updike.

2. A number of poets have had their works recorded. Use records and listen to artists reading their own poetry. Discuss and share reactions to the poet. What does the poet say about God, reason for living, creation, etc.? Most record shops stock these albums. A look through a record catalog will reveal many types of artists and their poetry. (Ask for the *Schwann* record catalog at your local record shop.)

3. Read the poetry of youth in church publications, school papers, etc. Also read the poetry of such "new" artists as Lawrence Ferlinghetti and Yevgeny Yevtushenko.

4. Have members of the group write poetry. Ask them to bring their material to a session for discussion. Encourage the creative response of the young people.

5. Ask a member of the local high school English department to discuss the latest trends and styles found in poetry. Have this person offer a historical perspective of poetry.

6. Study the poetry of church hymns. Do these forms of traditional music in the church still communicate to contemporary man? Were the poems of the hymn writers designed for an urbanized or rural world? Attempt to write lyrics for new hymns. Perhaps the group can develop poetic and meaningful hymns for its church and then submit these new hymns to denominational offices.

7. Conduct poetry reading sessions. Highlight the sessions with appropriate lighting, music, and colored slides. Combine the reading with sight and sound media to achieve a varied experience with the poem.

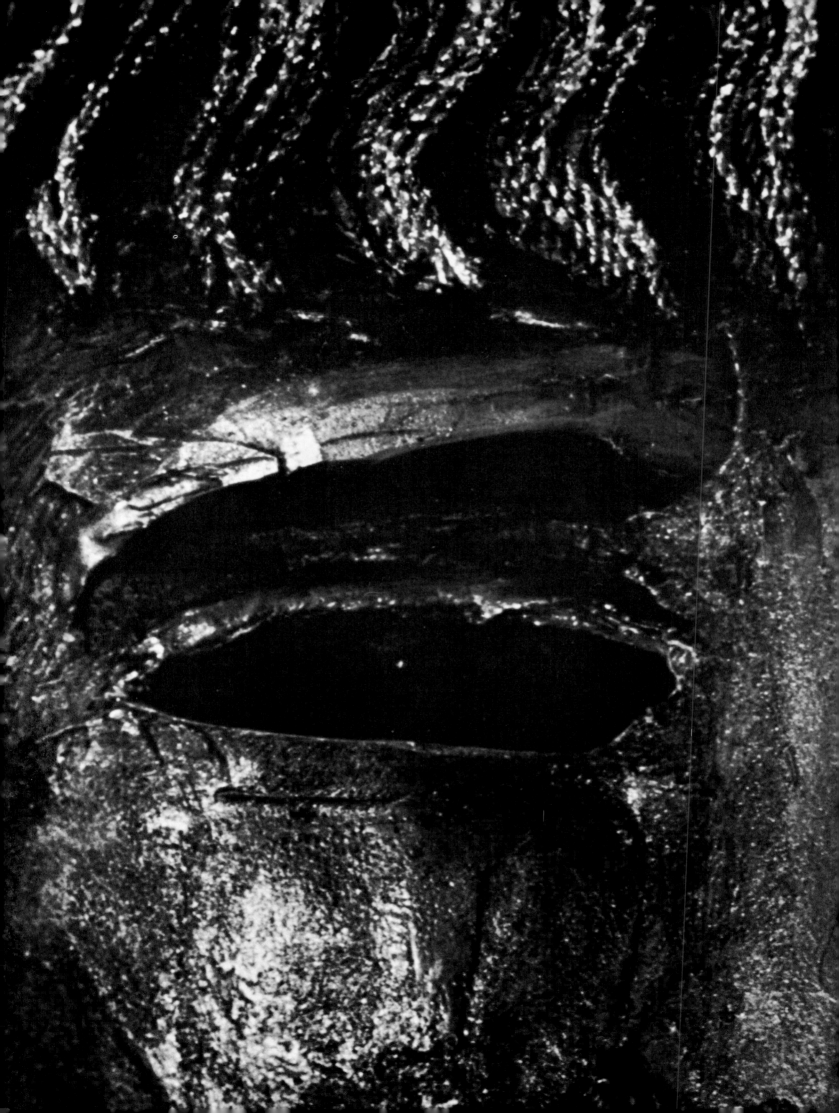

The Play's
The
Thing

"The cause of plagues is sinne, if you look to it well: and the cause of sinne are playes: therefore the cause of plagues are playes."

The above words were written by an unknown churchman in the 16th century. They represent the state of drama at one period in the history of the church. Although the Medieval church used drama extensively, it was later dropped as a communication media, as were most of the visual arts. Now the church again is discovering the rich value of dramatic art. More and more people within Christian congregations are turning to drama as a means of communication. Its rich dimension of portrayal has become a significant means of expressing the Gospel for those who recognize its powers. Since its key is conflict (ideas, people, actions, message, etc.), it can stimulate people to ask pertinent questions and provoke honest discussion in matters that are important to each of us.

The church should consider the use of quality drama as a resource to confront young people with live human situations because drama can help them see themselves and the human situation which surrounds them. It can open them to ideas and expose them to the interpretations and answers people are giving to life situations. Drama can open the way for Christians to bring the Gospel to life as it is lived in the world by looking at that life through the words and actions of the play. At the same time drama in the church ought not only be viewed, but its many possibilities for involvement ought to be employed in their various forms.

DRAMA IN THE PARISH MINISTRY

Kinds of Drama

Drama has many forms. It should be understood in a much broader perspective than simply a play being performed on a stage. Some of the large variety of forms which lend themselves to creative use in the church are the following.

Role Playing—Role playing allows a group to "act out" spontaneously a problem in human relations. The leader and group may then analyze their enactment in terms of the setting and the meaning of the Christian stance in that situation.

Play Reading—In this situation a group is chosen simply to read the play. A leader selects several people to be the "readers" in advance. Each person is given a copy of the play, and practice sessions are held in advance of the youth group session. Discussion follows the play reading.

Play Walking—This is similar to play reading except that the readers "walk through" the play, using simple props such as tables and chairs. This method adds motion to the play reading.

Choral Reading—A speaking choir is not often thought of as drama, but it is one of the rich varieties which can be used in youth group worship, congregational worship, and special congregational programs.

Creative Dance—This art form technically belongs with the dance, but it carries in it aspects of the drama. The creative rhythmic movements of the dance allows an individual to express thoughts, beliefs, feelings, and word interpretations. The creative dance has been used in church worship and is mentioned often in the Old Testament. Many artists and theologians consider the dance a "supreme symbol of spiritual life." Dancing is the loftiest, the most moving, the most beautiful of the arts because it is no mere translation; it is life itself! Perhaps it is one of the few pure art forms. An interpretive dance of the creation account in Genesis or the Lord's Prayer involves the entire body in a demonstration of witness and faith. This is undoubtedly the most difficult form of drama, and for that reason trained assistance such as a high school or college dance instructor may be needed.

Play Production—Besides the reading and discussing of plays, the youth group may share the power of drama by producing a play for the congregation, either in a quality production for the stage or in the form of an in-depth chancel drama. There is a rich variety of material available for both.

Happenings—A "happening" is a new form of theater providing creative approaches to drama. A "happening" is a dramatic collage with divers elements having no story line or plot form, yet each unrelated action has a total meaning or mood. A "happening" may combine the actions of music, film, slides, lighting, people, and staging, all designed to create a visual effect upon the viewer. In a "happening" many unrelated items and art forms are combined in order to create new meanings for old ideas. Many church groups have created "happenings." Any group seeking to do this for the first time would profit from consultation with the local high school drama teacher or from an approach to a community drama group for assistance.

DISCUSSING THE PLAY

(Discussion will vary according to the needs of a group, its size and its readiness for such a venture into drama. The leader should be free to adapt discussion material for his group.)

The discussion guide for "Focus on the Film" (see chapter of this book on film) can be adapted and used to discuss the play. The following information will aid in deeper understanding:

1. General discussion

a. Who is the protagonist? (character opposing antagonist)

b. Who is the antagonist? (character opposing the protagonist, creating discord)

c. What is the theme? (the main idea woven throughout the drama)

d. What is the central conflict? (may be within a character, between two characters, with other ideas. Essential to drama.)

e. What is the plot? (the story which is used to develop the theme)

f. What is the mood of the play?

g. Where is the suspense?

h. Where is the climax? (the mood of excitement or expectancy)

i. What important choices were made by the characters?

2. After analyzing the play move into the following areas:

a. Is the central struggle of the play a common one in real life?

b. What influences and background make the characters what they are?

c. Were influences good or evil? In which way? Why?

d. Is the ultimate choice of the main character a Christian choice? Is it practical? True to life? What other choices could be made? Is the solution probable? Were there alternate solutions?

3. Take a look at the characters.

a. Is the character dull, stupid, average, smart, brilliant?

b. Does the character have any Christian bearing or response in situations?

c. What is the character's attitude toward others?

d. Is the character willing to change? Seek ideas? Become a new person?

e. Is the character poised, changeable, gay, confident, confused, etc.?

f. What is the character's social and financial standing? His work?

g. Is there reflection of the character's home situation? Childhood? Church?

After a general discussion of the drama the group may divide into smaller sections to apply these and other questions to the play and its characters. Each group could bring summary reactions and further questions to the entire group.

ADDITIONAL GROUP STUDY SESSIONS

1. Listen to recorded performances of plays. Follow the play with scripts where possible. Excellent recordings are now available of *Death of a Salesman, Murder in the Cathedral, Cocktail Party, For Heaven's Sake, J. B.*, and many more. Paperback books of these scripts are available. Keep alert to the new dramas available on recordings. (Ask for a *Schwann* record catalog at your record shop.)

2. Visit and view local drama, either a major downtown production or a local "tenthouse" production. Return to the church building and discuss the play or discuss it in a booth at a local restaurant. If the high school produces a drama, perhaps the group can discuss the drama with the cast.

3. Invite a touring drama group into your congregation. The resource section below lists such traveling groups. Involve the actors in your discussion. Ask them to interpret and reflect upon the roles they assumed in the drama.

RESOURCES
Role Playing
Role Playing. Alan F. Klein.
Association Press.
291 Broadway, New York, N.Y. 10007

A scene from Shakespeare's "Richard III"
as presented at
Pennsylvania State University

A scene from Shakespeare's "Richard III"
as presented at
Pennsylvania State University

*A scene from Shakespeare's "Richard III"
as presented at
Pennsylvania State University*

Clinic on Role Playing. Bulletin issued by the Presbyterian Distribution Service, 156 Fifth Avenue, New York, New York 10010.

Choral Reading and Speaking
The following choral reading books are edited by Brown and Heltman and published by Westminster Press:
Choral Readings for Worship and Inspiration
Choral Readings from the Bible
Choral Readings for Teenage Worship and Inspiration
Great Bible Stories for the Verse Speaking Group
Choral Reading for Fun and Recreation
An additional book of value is *The Art of Choral Speaking* by Cecil de Bank, published by Walter H. Baker and Company, 100 Summer Street, Boston, Massachusetts 02110

Rhythmic Movement
The Art of the Rhythmic Choir. Margaret Taylor, 7 Fourth Street, Athens, Ohio.
Motion Choir (setting for Te Deum). Bulletin 10, Lutheran Society for Worship and the Arts, 2375 Como Avenue, St. Paul, Minnesota.

Plays
The Circle Beyond Fear. Darius Swann. Friendship Press.
For Heaven's Sake. Bakers Plays, 100 Summer Street, Boston, Massachusetts.
The Cup of Trembling (with discussion guide). Seabury Press.
The Visit of God (Christian portrait on Psalm 8). Norman Habel and Donald Busarow. Concordia Seminary Press, 801 De Mun Avenue, St. Louis, Missouri.
The Sign of Jonah. Guenter Rutenborn. Thomas Nelson and Sons.

The Crucible. Arthur Miller. Dramatists Play Service, 14 East 38th Street, New York, New York 10036.

Play Books
Religious Drama I. Marvin Halverson, editor. Meridian Books, Inc., New York, New York.
Plays are: "For the Time Being" (Auden); "The First Born" (Fry); "David" (Lawrence); "The Zeal of Thy House" (Sayers); "The Bloody Tenet" (Schevill).

Religious Drama II. E. Martin Browne, editor. Meridian Books, Inc., New York, New York.
Plays are: "The Creation of Man" (York); "The Garden of Eden" (York); "Noah's Flood" (Chester); "The Sacrifice of Isaac" (Brome manuscript); "The Temptation of Christ" (York); "Everyman"; and others.

Religious Drama III. Marvin Halverson, editor. Meridian Books, Inc., New York, New York.
Plays are: "The Last Word" (Broughton); "The House by the Stable" and "Grab and Grace" (Williams); "Santa Claus" (Cummings); "Let Men Live" (Lagerkvist); "Billy Budd" (Coxe and Chapman); "The Gospel Witch" (Phelps).

Treasure of Religious Plays. Thelma Sharman Brown, Association Press.
Plays are: "A Christmas Carol" (Dickens); "White Christmas" (Wilson); "A Child Is Born" (Benet); "No Room in the Hotel" (Wilson); "The Symbol of the Cross" (Shannon); "Empty Hands" (Clark); "Among Thieves" (Clark); and many others.

Saint Anne and the Gouty Rector and Other Plays. Henri Gheon and Henri Brochet. Longman's Green and Company, New York, New York.

A collection of plays by one of France's foremost literary figures of this country. The plays, which are modeled on medieval mystery and miracle forms, are geared to contemporary characterizations and current problems. Production notes accompany the play.
Plays are: "Saint Anne and the Gouty Rector"; "The Gardener Who Was Afraid of Death"; "The Sausage Maker's Interlude"; "The Poor Man Who Died Because He Wore Gloves"; "Parade at the Devil's Bridge"; "Christmas at the Crossroads"; "Saint Felix and His Potatoes."

Better Plays for Today's Churches. Selected by John Bachman and E. Martin Browne. Association Press.
A collection of twelve modern religious plays depicting themes from modern society, the Passion events, Christmas, and Old Testament themes. Included in the book are "Christ in the Concrete City" (Phillip Turner) and "Go Down Moses" (Philip Lamb).

Great Christian Plays. Edited by Switz and Johnson, Seabury Press.
A book of classical religious plays and selected choral readings.

Youth Programs (Drama Section), Volumes 12, 14, 15, 16.
Office of Youth Ministries, 875 North Dearborn Street, Chicago, Illinois 60610 ($1.50 each, single copy; $1.25 each, three or more).
Shorter dramas on varying themes for the youth ministry.

Coventry Porch Plays. Baker Plays, Boston, Massachusetts.
Plays are: "This Is the End"; "The Site"; "Who Is There to Ask."

4 Contemporary Religious Plays.
Paulist Press, Glen Rock, New Jersey.
Plays from *Look Up and Live* (CBS-TV) and *The Catholic Hour* (NBC-TV).
Plays are: "The Shadow of the Valley"; "Once There Was A Postman"; "The Broken Pitcher"; "Without the Angels."

The Delinquent, The Hipster and the Square. Alva I. Cox, editor. Bethany Press, St. Louis, Missouri. Series of plays from *Look Up and Live* (CBS-TV).
Plays are: "The Delinquent"; "The Hipster"; "The Square"; "Human Relations"; "God and Prayer"; "Death."

Modern Monologues for Young People.
John Murray. Plays Incorporated, Boston, Massachusetts.

Christmas Plays and Programs.
Ailean Fischer. Plays Incorporated, Boston, Massachusetts.

The Seeking Years. John M. Gunn, editor. Bethany Press, St. Louis, Missouri.
Series of plays from *Look Up and Live* (CBS-TV).
Plays are: "No Man Is an Island"; "A Thing of Beauty"; "The Will to Win"; "Plenty of Rain"; "The Puzzle"; "The Faith Hawker."

Armour of Light. John W. Bloch, Bethany Press, St. Louis, Missouri.
Series of plays from *Look Up and Live* (CBS-TV).
Plays are: "On the Rocks"; "The Peddler"; "The Speaking Foot"; "The Wide Door."

TECHNICAL RESOURCE MATERIALS
International Journal of Religious Education, "Drama in Christian Education," Box 303, New York, New York 10027.

Religious Drama: Ends and Means.
Harold Ehrensperger. Abingdon, 1962.
$6.00.

Touted as the authoritative volume of all facets and phases of religious drama. Most useful for parish concerns for religious drama.

The Key to Good Church Drama.
James S. Kerr. Augsburg Publishing House, 426 South Fifth Street, Minneapolis, Minnesota 55415. 1964.
$1.95.
A small 71-page practical guide for drama in the church. The volume gives hard-core help from the time of selecting a play, casting, and rehearsals to the technical sides of staging a play with words for its director.

Methods of Drama in Christian Education. Board of Christian Education, The United Presbyterian Church, U.S.A., Witherspoon Building, Philadelphia, Pennsylvania 19107.

Improvisation for the Theater.
Viola Spolin. Northwestern University Press, Evanston, Illinois.

Happenings. Michael Kirby. A Dutton Paperback, New York, New York.

PLAY PUBLISHERS
Abingdon Press, New York, and Nashville, Tennessee.

Association Press, 291 Broadway, New York, New York 10007.

Walter H. Baker Company (Baker's Plays), 100 Summer Street, Boston, Massachusetts 12110.

Bethany Press, Box 179, 2640 Pine Blvd., St. Louis, Missouri 63166.

Broadman Press, 127 9th Avenue N., Nashville, Tennessee 37203

Dramatic Publishing Company, 179 North Michigan Avenue, Chicago, Illinois.

Dramatists Play Service, Inc., 14 E. 38th Street, New York, New York 10016.

Eldridge Publishing Company, Franklin, Ohio, and Denver, Colorado.

Fortress Press, 2900 Queen Lane, Philadelphia, Pennsylvania 19129

John Knox Press, 8 N. 6th Street, Box 1176, Richmond, Virginia 23209

Judson Press, Valley Forge, Pennsylvania.

Macmillan Publishing Company, 866 Third Avenue, New York, New York 10022

Oxford University Press, 417 5th Avenue, New York, New York 10016

Plays, Inc., 8 Arlington Street, Boston, Massachusetts 02116

Religious Drama Society, 166 Shaftesbury Avenue, London W. C. 2, England.

Seabury, 815 Second Avenue, New York, New York 10017

Seminary Drama Society, Concordia Seminary, 801 DeMun, St. Louis, Missouri.

Standard Publishing Company, 8121 Hamilton Avenue, Cincinnati, Ohio 45231.

Wetmore Declamation Bureau, Sioux City, Iowa.

Zondervan Publishing House, Grand Rapids, Michigan.

TRAVELING DRAMA GROUPS
The Theater of Concern, Mr. Norman Dietz, 18 Jacobus Place, New York, New York 10063.

The Chicagoland Lutheran Theatre, Room 705, 343 South Dearborn Street, Chicago, Illinois

Cross and Crown Players, Valparaiso University, Valparaiso Indiana.

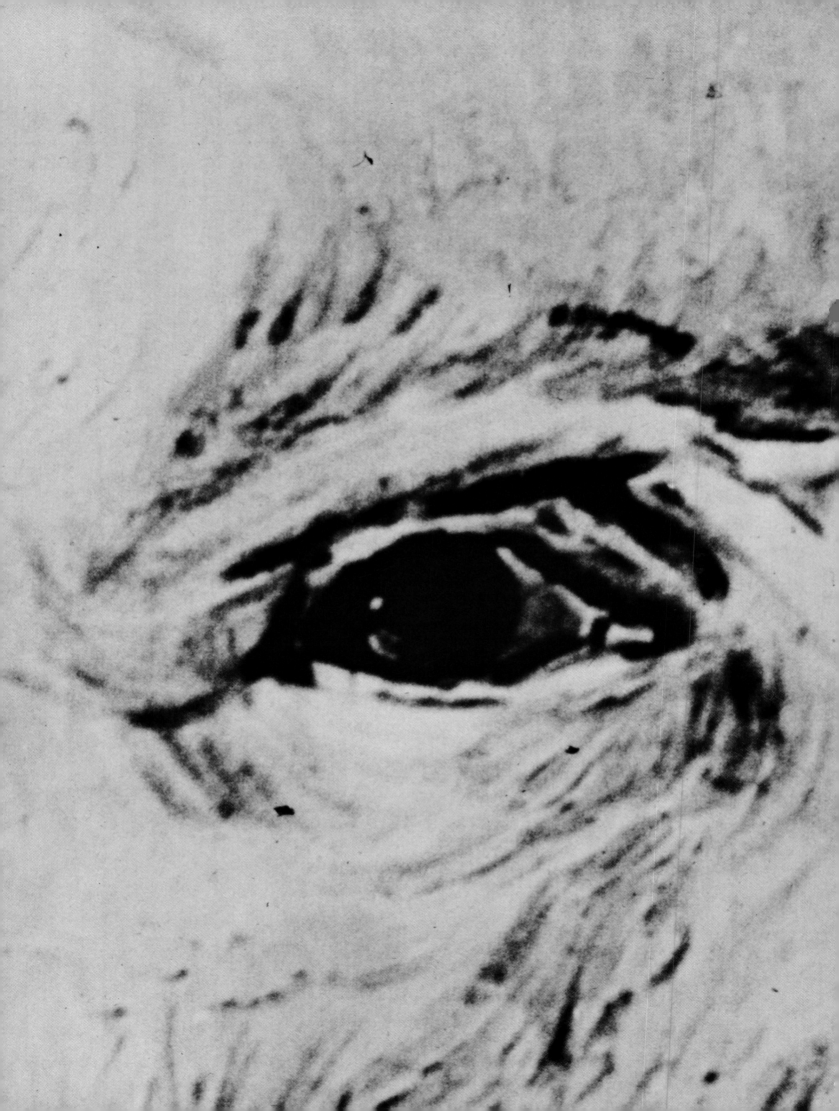

"WINDFALL"
a color intaglio
by Bruce Shobaken

Cincinnati Museum of Art,
Cincinnati, Ohio.

Cleveland Museum of Art,
Cleveland, Ohio.

Museum of Modern Art,
11 West 53rd Street,
New York, New York 10019.

National Gallery of Art,
Washington, D.C. 20025

Walker Art Center,
1710 Lyndale Avenue South,
Minneapolis, Minnesota 55403.

Magazines
Arts Magazine, Art Digest, Inc.,
41 East 57th Street,
New York, New York 10022. $9.50/yr.

Christian Art,
1801 West Greenleaf Avenue,
Chicago, Illinois 60626. $5.00/yr.

*International Journal of Religious
Education,* Box 303 New York,
New York 10027. This magazine offers
two issues which deal with the arts,
"Art in Christian Education" and
"Contemporary Art and Christian
Education." 75c each.

Books
*Christian Faith and the Contemporary
Arts.* Finley Eversole, editor. Abingdon
Press. $5.00.

*Christianity, the Arts and Contemporary
Culture.* Mildred Tonge. A study docu-
ment published by the Department of
Worship and the Arts of the National
Council of Churches, 475 Riverside
Drive, New York, New York 10027.

Nature and Grace in Art.
University of North Carolina Press. $7.50.

Christianity in Modern Art.
Frank and Dorothy Getlein.
Bruce. 1959. $4.50.

The Pocket Dictionary of Art Terms
Edited by Mervyn Levy.
New York Graphic Society,
Greenwich, Connecticut. 1961. 95c.

The Meaning of Art. Herbert Read.
Pelican Book. $1.45.

*Report of the Special Committee on the
Council's Role in the Field of Religion
and the Arts.* National Council of
Churches, 475 Riverside Drive,
New York, New York 10027.

Art Exhibits
The National Council of Churches pro-
vides a traveling art exhibition for
congregations. Write to the NCC office
(above) for information relating
to this exhibit.

Filmstrip and Record
Modern Art and The Gospel. United
Church Press, Philadelphia, Pennsylvania. An excellent presentation related
to the interpretation and meaning of
modern art from a Christian perspective.
A color filmstrip and record (40 minutes) with user's guide, biographical
notes, and suggestions for further study.

Also
Art in the USA and Where to Find it.
"Arts Magazine," 41 East 57th Street,
New York, New York 10019. A gallery
directory which serves as a guide to
the best of art in the nation. $1.25.

Renewal
In the church

The renewal of the arts in our society requires that the church also restore the arts to their rightful place in the Christian community. Art, as an expression of man and as a communication media, needs to be understood before we can begin meaningful exchange with the forms. An arts festival will expose members of the congregation and community to the artist, his work, and his message, as well as our interpretation and response. The arts festival ought not be thought of as an "evangelistic" effort or "propaganda" thrust, but rather as man's effort to speak to the world and to the church. Hopefully, the arts will be shared for the purpose and joy of man's participation in creation as well as understanding and growth of those who view the art forms.

PURPOSE OF AN ARTS FESTIVAL

It is important to define the goals and objectives of your arts festival. A congregation ought to know why they want an arts festival as well as what they hope to accomplish through it in terms of the congregation and the community. The reasons will vary in different situations depending upon the location of the congregation (inner city, suburban, college community, rural) as well as the level of the congregation to participate in and have sensitivity for the arts. The following are goals which may be expanded to fit local needs:

1. Offer members of the congregation and community (children, youth, adults) an exposure to the arts (the expression of man's spirit as he responds to God and the world about him) in order that they may comprehend to some degree the artist's message to the church and the Christian in a changing society.

2. Cultivate an interest and participation in the arts by members of the congregation so that they may understand art sufficiently to involve themselves in dialogue with the artist.

3. Open avenues of participation in God's creation where the creative abilities of members of the congregation may be shared.

4. Communicate the concepts and meanings of the arts to members of the congregation in order that they may understand the good in the traditional and the message and sensitivity of the contemporary.

STYLES OF ARTS FESTIVALS

An arts festival may take shape in varying styles. Whichever form, from the simplest to the most complex, it ought to reflect quality planning and development.

1. *Congregation Arts Festival.* This is the simplest form of arts festival. It involves the creative abilities of the members of the congregation. Participation in this event could be by children, youth, and adults. This festival should include only original works by members of the congregation, avoiding the "paint-the-number" type exercises. Included in the exhibits should be the traditional types of art as well as collages, films, etc. Avoid any atmosphere of contest with judging. However, a professional artist of the community could comment upon the techniques used and offer constructive assistance to each of the participants.

2. *Professional Arts Festival.* In this festival the professional talents of the local community or geographical area should be used. This kind of festival requires a small group to meet with the artist and select the works for the artist to display. The advantage of this festival is that it permits the artist the opportunity to speak to the congregation and engage in dialogue with its members. Art shops and salons are often willing to

assist such a project by loaning works of art to a congregation. Another advantage of this kind of exhibit is that the works of the artist often are for sale, thus offering the congregation opportunity to have works of art in their homes.

3. *Traveling Exhibitions.* This is a ready-made exhibit of quality material which contains enough material for a full arts festival. Often the local college, high school, library, or arts society has such exhibits.

4. *Full Arts Festival.* This style festival includes all forms of art—drama, painting, sculpture, film, creative dance, etc. It is the most detailed and perhaps the most exciting of arts festivals. Often churches of the community have combined to sponsor this type of festival jointly, with each handling a specific art form. A complete festival of this type requires at least a year's preparation.

PREPARING FOR THE ARTS FESTIVAL

No matter which style of festival a congregation selects, each requires thoughtful preparation. It is best to select a committee to do the initial work and develop the festival. Committee make-up ought to include members of the congregation who are sensitive to the arts. Additional assistance can come from a local high school or college instructor. The minister of the congregation might serve as advisory member of the committee.

An important function of the committee is publicity. Public relations include releases to the local newspapers, radio and television stations, and church papers. Posters will be needed for local places of business, libraries, schools, churches, etc. Local community leaders and art societies should also be invited. Personal invitations ought to be sent to members of the congregations. Additional invitations should be made available to members so that they may send them to their friends.

Arts Festival

64

*Typical arrangement for hanging
paintings and making stands for
sculpture.*

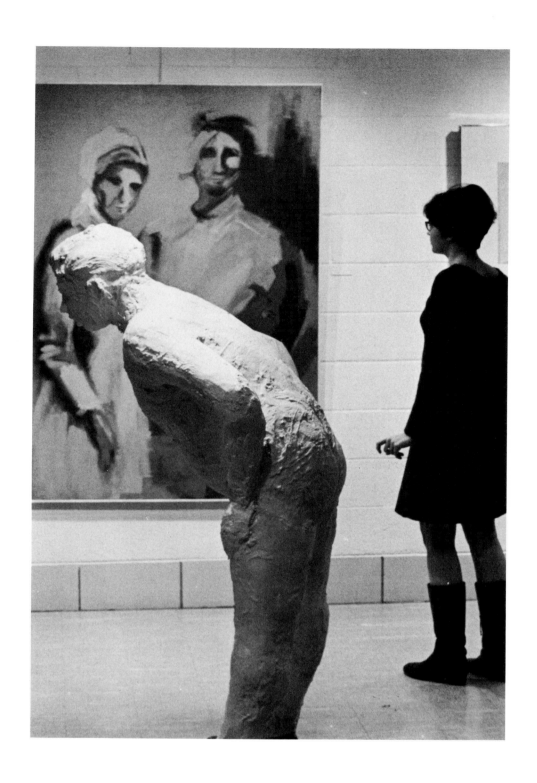

ARTS FESTIVAL CHECK LIST

Insurance. Most artists are concerned that their works be insured by the group sponsoring the festival. Very often it is possible to contact the church's insurance company and attach a "rider" to the present policy for the time of the festival.

Finances. Financing an arts festival is of key importance to the quality desired. A budget should be prepared for adoption by the committee early in the planning. Money can be raised through freewill offerings at special worship services. The church may allocate a portion of its budget for the festival. Groups within the church may share a portion of their treasury with the festival. The patron system is an excellent means of securing financial assistance. The patron system offers people the choice of several specific amounts to give to the festival (choice: $5.00, $10.00, $15.00). The patrons would be listed on the festival program. Additional contributions might be solicited from those who attend the festival.

Display Area. Setting up the display area is in itself a work of art. Contact a local display company or art studio to assist with the arrangement of the exhibit. (Enclosed toward the end of the section of this book are some hints for displaying the art.)

Programs. It is advisable to produce a program listing the events of the festival as well as a listing of the works of art displayed. Ads may be placed in the booklet to help defray expenses. The listing of works of art should take the following form:

#5 *Christ Before Pilate*
(number of display and title)
Georges Roualt (name of artist)
Colored Lithograph (art form or technique)
Mr. Joseph Randall Smith (owner of the work)

(If the work is for sale the price may be listed in place of the owner's name.)

Equipment. It is absolutely necessary to have all equipment at hand and in working order for all festival events. Lecterns, film projectors, seating arrangements, public address system, etc., need to be in a state of readiness prior to any particular event for which the equipment is needed.

Clean-up. Dismantling of the festival displays and the return of all works to proper sources is as important as the preparation for the event. Letters of acknowledgment are to be sent to all participants and helpers of the festival.

Evaluation. The most important item for any event is the evaluation. Glance back and make a critical evaluation of the event. List strong points as well as the areas which need change. Share the evaluation with the congregation's governing board as well as next year's arts festival committee.

Hopefully, an arts festival will lead the congregation into an experience of growth and renewal as the members confront the prophetic and priestly arts festival committee.

ARTS FESTIVAL PROGRAM

The following outline offers a sample of an arts festival program. Such a program will vary according to scope, facilities, and style of festival planned.

SUNDAY
Sunday morning
—Festival worship
Sunday afternoon
—Exhibition opening and tea
Sunday evening
—Exhibition, dialogue with visiting artist(s)

MONDAY
Monday afternoon
—Exhibition
Monday evening
—Exhibition

—Film program (a program of short films lasting approximately 45 minutes can be shown three times this evening.) (Note the sample film program at the conclusion of this outline entitled "Counter-Tempo XX")

TUESDAY
Tuesday afternoon
—Exhibition
Tuesday evening
—Exhibition
—Chancel drama presentation and discussion

WEDNESDAY
Wednesday afternoon
—Exhibition
Wednesday evening
—Exhibition
—Special worship services involving new forms, including music and creative dance

THURSDAY
Thursday afternoon
—Exhibition
Thursday evening
—Exhibition
—Discussion of the arts in other media (TV, film, comics, literature)

SATURDAY
Saturday morning and afternoon
—Exhibition (special emphasis on children's art)

SUNDAY
Sunday morning
—Special worship of celebration involving some of the arts (procession with banners, choir, creative dance, etc.)
Sunday afternoon
—Final showing of exhibit

A SAMPLE FILM PROGRAM FOR AN ARTS FESTIVAL

Counter — Tempo XX

The shorter documentary-style film has come into its own during the past ten years. The creative challenge of this type film is being met by professional producers, college students, and high school youth. Film festivals, geared to the shorter film, are cropping up throughout the world. Each year the University of Michigan at Ann Arbor and the University of California at Los Angeles sponsor film festivals for student produced films.

We title this sample film program "Counter—Tempo XX." The films suggested here offer commentary on the 20th century. Using science and art as a two-edged sword, these films offer a view of the century—a century unique for its amazing advances in science as well as its tragic acts of war and hate. These films offer commentary on both the joy and the sorrow of our century. *(Credit is given to producers when available. The cost listed following the credit line is rental fee for one showing. Sources are listed at the end of the review.)*

1. *AUTOMANIA 2000* (Directed by John Hales, written by Joy Batchelor, animated by Harold Shitaker. England. $12.50—10 minutes)
This film offers a satire on today's trend toward increased productivity of consumer goods through science and research. If you think the population explosion is a problem, you should see the year 2000 when the cars learn to reproduce themselves. The ultimate in automation produces a world covered by layers of cars with people living caveman-style in the various layers.

2. *NIGHT AND FOG* (Directed by Alain Resnais, script by Jean Cayrel. France. $30.00—31 minutes).
The term "night and fog" was first used by Adolph Hitler to describe the fate of certain prisoners. They were to disappear into the night and fog without even a trace of their burial place. The camps and the death of nine million people are the subject matter of this short film. Through a journey in black and white as well as color, we experience the horror of the concentration camps of the 40's and their visual springlike beauty (delicate posies growing by brick ovens) in the 60's. It is not a film of hatred or reminiscence, but rather a film of disquietude.

3. *IT'S ABOUT THIS CARPENTER* ($7.50—14 minutes).
This is a film replete with symbolism. Imagine Christ carrying a cross through midtown Manhattan. Pretty startling! This film depicts a young, bearded carpenter delivering a huge cross to a church. On this journey he encounters all sorts of individuals. Some of the people find the sign humorous, others are antagonistic, and some (including a clergyman playing the organ) ignore him. One of the most interesting scenes show the carpenter carrying the cross through a parade, completely ignored. What if the man were Jesus Christ? Would the situation be the same? Perhaps he is; perhaps it is!!

4. *THE CRITIC* (Produced by Ernest Pintoff, created and narrated by Mel Brooks, animated by Bob Heath. U.S.A. Approximately $8.00—5 minutes).
A very funny film which pokes fun at abstract art and its cohorts who appear to alienate the "average man in the street." *The Critic* is an anonymous voice in an art theater interpreting and protesting the weird arty shapes on the screen. "What's dis? Dis is nice; dis is cute." *The Critic* suggests that the artist could probably do something useful like driving a truck or making a shoe. The words of *The Critic* have probably been in the back of our minds at times while visiting art galleries or attending concerts. Some have even suggested *The Critic* is the institutionalized church looking at the world, or vice versa.

5. *21—87* (Arthur Lipsett. Canada. $5.00—10 minutes).
In this film we view everyman—and no man! In this production Lipsett matches

his earlier film, *Very Nice, Very Nice.*
Through a montage of film clips we
experience man waiting for his number
to come up. Unless his number does come
up he is predestined to be unnoticed
and unknown. What's your number?

6. *ALF, BILL, AND FRED*
(Produced by Robert Godfrey. England.
$15.00—10 minutes).
Happiness is a good film. Through good
art and magazine clips the film comments on the meaning of being a "swing-
er" in society. What changes man?
Money? Friends? A duck, a dog, and a
humorous man find themselves
in this dilemma.

7. *BLIND GARY DAVIS*
(Harold Becker. U.S.A.
$12.50—11 minutes)
Gary Davis, known to the folk tune
world, sings the blues in a native and
poetic manner. As he sings we view the
faces of the city streets. Davis' songs
serve as a counterpoint for images of
man and the world. As the last song is
sung, "Death Don't Have No Mercy,"
the camera picks out its victims. A
powerful portrayal of the sensitivity
of the camera and the struggle of man.

8. *ORANGE AND BLUE* (Peter and
Clare Chermayeff, music by Joseph
Raposo, produced at the Film Study
Center of Harvard University. U.S.A.
$10.00—15 minutes).
This last film ends our program, *Counter-
Tempo XX,* with a child's dream-world
bursting into freedom, sensing both the
gaiety and the serious overtones of life.
The film centers on two lifelike balls,
one orange, one blue. They bounce
from the innocence and beauty of nature
into a junkyard and war surplus depot.
In the action of the balls we see delight-
ful moods of adventure, curiosity, coy-
ness, and gladness. As the balls are
overwhelmed by the visual terror of the
junkyard and surplus depot, we experience the pangs of confusion and fear.
A delight to view, a challenge for conversation, particularly the ending when
the two balls retreat into their simple life.

Sources:
Films 1, 2, 4, 5, 6, 7, 8:
Contemporary Films, Inc.
East　　　—267 West 25th Street,
　　　　　New York, New York 10001.
Midwest—828 Custer Avenue,
　　　　　Evanston, Illinois 60202.
West　　—1211 Polk Street,
　　　　　San Francisco,
　　　　　California 94109.
Film 3: *Mass Media Ministries,*
2116 North Charles Street,
Baltimore, Maryland.

SETTING UP THE DISPLAY

1. Reserve a room for the art display,
clearing out all distractions to the exhibit.
This includes dirty walls and windows
as well as old pictures on the wall.

2. The room should be well lighted. If
poorly lighted, import proper lighting.
Keep the lighting soft, not harsh.

3. For insurance purposes the room
should be kept locked when
not exhibiting.

4. If possible, limit the display to one
room. Avoid spreading the display
throughout the church.

5. Sculptures should rest on individual
stands. Small tables will do in place
of stands. If time and money permit,
wooden rectangles or cubes may be
constructed on which to place the sculptures. Paint the stands black or white.

6. Graphics may be hung on the wall
or on special display boards. The display
boards can be easily constructed and
used for other purposes throughout the
year. The boards should be painted
an off-white.

7. Arrange display panels in order to
use light to best advantage. Arrange the
display to have an "opening panel" available for viewing when guests enter the
exhibit. The opening panel should be
appealing; it sets the theme for the
exhibit. At the opening panel you may
want to have one selection of art which
capsules the theme, also a guest book
and festival statement. Insure a good
"traffic pattern" that people may easily
walk past all art pieces. Don't make a
maze but leave easy exits (even for
those who dislike the showing).

8. Arrange for a few chairs to be
placed about for older people to rest.

9. Arrange to have five or six large floor
plants to add some life to the exhibit
and freshness to the room. Make arrangement pleasing and complimentary to the
exhibit. Florists, with proper acknowledgment in the program, are generally
willing to loan such plants to an exhibit.

10. If at all possible, work with an
artist (or commercial window
arranger) to set up the display.
Quality art is often less appealing
when displayed poorly.